The Ultimate Illustrated Bathroom Reader Volume 2

1,000 Fascinating Facts to Entertain, Amuse, and Educate All Ages

David Fickes

Introduction

I have tried to ensure that all the information in this book is as accurate as possible. This book is intended for people who prefer to read interesting facts rather than quiz themselves.

There are 1,000 fascinating facts with 96 black-and-white photographs covering a wide range of topics including animals, arts, history, literature, movies, science and nature, sports, television, U.S. geography, U.S. presidents, world geography, and more.

If you enjoyed this book and learned a little and would like others to enjoy it also, please put out a review or rating. If you scan the QR code below, it will take you directly to the Amazon review and rating page.

1) The Great Pyramid of Giza has eight sides; each of the four sides is split from base to tip by slight concave indentations, creating eight sides. The indentations were first noticed in 1940 by a pilot flying over.

2) Iceland's phone book is alphabetized by first name. Everyone is referenced by their first name, and they don't have surnames in the traditional sense. Their surname is their father's first name suffixed with either son or daughter.

3) Rascette lines are the creases on your inner wrist.

4) Whales, dolphins, orcas, and porpoises have an unusual form of sleep called unihemispheric slow-wave sleep. They shut down one hemisphere of their brain and close the opposite eye. During this time, the other half of the brain monitors what is happening in their environment and controls breathing functions. Dolphins will sometimes hang motionless at the surface of the water during sleep, or they may swim slowly.

5) Research indicates that everyone dreams, whether they remember doing so or not.

6) The busiest muscles in the human body are in the eyes; it is estimated that they move 100,000 times a day.

7) The pronghorn antelope is the second-fastest land animal; pronghorns can achieve speeds of 55 mph.

8) The zombie ant fungi can hijack an ant's central nervous and force the ant to do what it wants. When an ant contacts the fungal spores, the fungus infects the ant and quickly spreads throughout its body. Fungal cells in the ant's head release chemicals that hijack the ant's central nervous system. The fungus forces the ant to climb up vegetation and clamp down onto a leaf or twig before killing it. After the ant is dead, the fungus grows a spore releasing stalk out of the back of the ant's head that infects more ants on the ground below.

9) The largest currency denomination ever printed in the United States is the 1934 $100,000 bill, featuring a picture of Woodrow Wilson. It was only printed for three weeks in December 1934 and January 1935, and they were only used for official transactions between Federal Reserve Banks.

10) If you weigh 150 pounds on the earth, you will weigh 4,200 pounds on the sun.

11) The average human body has 30-40 trillion cells, and over 80% of them are red blood cells.

12) The primary reason dog noses are wet is because dogs secrete mucus that aids their sense of smell.

13) Squirrels cause about 10-20% of all power outages in the United States. Squirrel outages tend to be more localized and more quickly fixed than those caused by storms.

14) The Big Dipper isn't a constellation; it is an asterism. There are 88 official constellations in the night sky; any other grouping of stars that isn't one of the 88 is an asterism. In the Big Dipper's case, it is part of the Ursa Major (Great Bear) constellation.

15) In 1879, Liege, Belgium, attempted to use 37 cats as mail carriers. Messages were placed in waterproof bags the cats carried around their necks. Not surprisingly, the cats proved to be unreliable and slow, taking many hours or a day to deliver the mail, and the service didn't last long.

16) If you smoothed out all the wrinkles in your brain, it would lie flat about the size of a pillowcase.

17) In a short spurt, a domestic cat can run up to 30 mph; the fastest speed a human has ever run is about 28 mph.

18) Since 2016, it has been illegal in France for supermarkets to throw away edible food; they must donate it to charities.

19) In 1870, the first African American was elected to serve in the U.S. Congress; he was a senator from Mississippi.

20) Desynchronosis is the technical term for jet lag.

21) In about 1000 AD, Norse explorer Leif Erikson arrived in continental North America, approximately 500 years before Christopher Columbus.

22) The giant and colossal squid's eye is up to 11 inches in diameter, the largest of any animal.

23) Some expensive perfumes still contain whale poop. Ambergris, a waxy substance produced in the intestines of sperm whales, has been incorporated in perfumes for a long time as a binding agent; it helps the fragrance linger on the skin and intensifies the scent of the perfume. It has now been mostly replaced by synthetic alternatives.

24) Australia has the largest population of poisonous snakes of any country.

25) Wendy's hamburgers are square because founder Dave Thomas took the phrase "not cutting corners" seriously, and he wanted the burgers to be square because the patties stick out of the bun in a way that showcases the meat's quality.

26) Mead is the oldest, widely-popular, alcoholic beverage. It is made from honey and was popular as far back as 2000 BC.

27) Hitler, Stalin, and Mussolini were all nominated for the Nobel Peace Prize.

28) Typewriter is the longest English word that can be made using the letters on only one row of a standard keyboard.

29) Psychologist William Marston was one of the inventors of the polygraph and created the character Wonder Woman and her Lasso of Truth.

30) During WWII due to a lack of anti-tank weapons, the Soviet Union used dogs strapped with explosives against German tanks. The machine guns on German tanks were too high to reach the low-running suicide dogs, and the Germans couldn't easily emerge from their tanks to shoot the dogs. The dogs were trained to go under the tanks and helped destroy over 300 tanks.

31) Snapping shrimp can snap their specialized claw shut producing a cavitation bubble that releases a sound as loud as 218 decibels, louder than a rocket launch. When the bubble collapses, it can reach temperatures of 4,700 degrees Celsius, almost as hot as the surface of the sun.

32) Except for sloths and manatees, all mammals have seven neck vertebrae.

33) The division sign (short horizontal line with a dot above and below) in math is called an obelus.

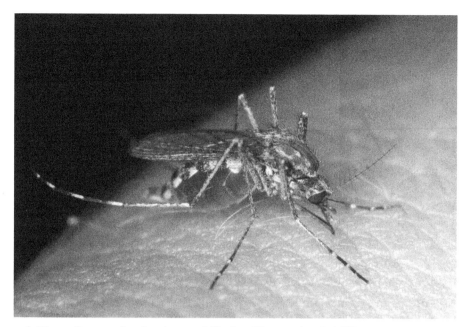

34) Mosquitos are by far the world's deadliest animal, killing over 700,000 people annually worldwide primarily from malaria. Snakes are the second-most deadly animal, killing about 50,000 people; dogs are third, killing about 25,000 people mainly through rabies. Crocodiles are the deadliest of the large animals, killing about 1,000 people. The hippopotamus is the deadliest large land mammal, killing an estimated 500 people annually.

35) Richard Nixon once carried three pounds of marijuana for Louis Armstrong. In 1958, Vice President Richard Nixon ran into Louis Armstrong at Idlewild Airport in New York. Since he didn't have to go through customs, Nixon offered to carry Armstrong's luggage. Without knowing it, Nixon carried three pounds of marijuana for Armstrong.

36) When Lord Byron became a student at Cambridge, dogs were prohibited, so he got a bear as a pet. The bear stayed in his lodgings, and Byron would take him for walks around the grounds.

37) Depending on conditions, the lifespan of a housefly is 15-30 days.

38) As soon as sand tiger shark embryos develop teeth while still in the womb, the largest of the embryos in each of the two uteruses attacks and eats its siblings, leaving just two pups to be born.

39) You could fit 1.3 million Earths inside the Sun, an average-size star.

40) A mouse's sperm is bigger than an elephant's sperm. Large animals tend to have large numbers of smaller sperm.

41) Abraham Lincoln's son Robert is the only person known to have witnessed the assassination of three U.S. presidents; he witnessed the assassinations of his father, James A. Garfield, and William McKinley.

42) Due to the Mpemba Effect, hot water may freeze faster than cold water. It still isn't clearly understood why.

43) Without your pinky finger, you would lose 50% of your hand strength.

44) Horses can't vomit. They have very strong lower esophageal sphincters that make it impossible for the valve to open under backward pressure from the stomach.

45) About 1 in 2,000 human babies are born with a tooth, known as a natal tooth.

46) When you read to yourself, your tongue and vocal cords still get movement signals from the brain. The process is known as subvocal speech and is characterized by minuscule movements in the larynx and other muscles involved in the articulation of speech; the movements are undetectable without the aid of machines.

47) Today's British accent first appeared among the British upper class about the time of the American Revolution. Before that, the British sounded like Americans.

48) David is the most frequently mentioned name in the bible; Jesus is second.

49) The Pilgrims didn't first land at Plymouth Rock; they first landed in what is now Provincetown, Massachusetts, and signed the Mayflower Compact there. They arrived at Plymouth Rock five weeks later.

50) Neil Armstrong didn't say, "one small step for man" when he set foot on the moon. He said, "one small step for a man." That is what Armstrong claims he said, and audio analysis confirms it. It has been misquoted all these years.

51) The Antarctic ice sheet has 90% of the earth's fresh water; it is equivalent to about 230 feet of water in the world's oceans.

52) Leatherback sea turtles have a third eye on the top of their head that allows them to detect night-day and seasonal cycles. The pink spot on their heads has very thin layers of bone and cartilage that allow light to pass through to the pineal gland in their brain that acts as a biological clock regulating night-day and seasonal cycles. It acts as a skylight, letting the turtles detect the subtle changes in sunlight from changing seasons.

53) Alfred Hitchcock appeared in more than 30 Alfred Hitchcock films.

54) Three-digit emergency phone numbers were first introduced in London in 1937. After a fire killed five people and the person calling for the fire brigade was kept waiting by the operator, they implemented the original 999 number.

55) Written out in English (one, two, three, etc.), eight is the first number alphabetically, no matter how high you go.

56) Wells Fargo has an ATM in McMurdo Station, Antarctica. A maintenance person shows up to service it every two years.

57) In 1932, Mildred "Babe" Didrikson won the team championship single-handedly at the AAU national track and field meet. She competed in 8 out of 10 events; she won five and tied for first in a sixth event. She won the team championship, despite being the only member of her team.

58) The television Emmy awards get their name from a tube used in early cameras. Image orthicon tubes were called immys, and the name was feminized to Emmy to match the female statuette.

59) The opossum has more teeth, 50, than any other land mammal.

60) Roman charioteer Gaius Appuleius Diocles, who lived in the 2nd century, was one of the most celebrated ancient athletes and might be the best-paid athlete of all time. He raced four-horse chariots, and records show he won 1,462 out of the 4,257 races he competed in. He also seemed to be a showman, making many of his victories come from behind last-second victories that made him even more popular. He raced for 24 years and retired at age 42. His winnings amounted to the equivalent of 2,600 kilograms of gold; considering the buying power at the time, that would make him a multi-billionaire in today's dollars.

61) The Fahrenheit and Celsius temperature scales are the same at 40 degrees below zero.

62) The longest earthworm is South African Microchaetus rappi; they can grow as long as 22 feet and average about 6 feet.

63) At President Andrew Jackson's funeral in 1845, his pet parrot was removed for swearing.

64) The hippopotamus is responsible for the most human deaths of any of the large African animals.

65) When the Gregorian calendar replaced the Julian calendar, 10 days were skipped; October 4, 1582, was followed by October 15, 1582, to get the calendar back on track with the position of the sun.

66) Hawaiian pizza is Canadian; it was invented in 1962 in Ontario, Canada.

67) The oldest surviving photograph was taken in 1826 by French photography pioneer Joseph Nicéphore Niépce. It is the view from the window of an estate in Burgundy, France; it was taken with an eight-hour exposure and was made on a pewter plate.

68) The largest private home ever built in the United States is the Biltmore Estate in Asheville, North Carolina. It was built for George Washington Vanderbilt II and was completed in 1895; it is 175,856 square feet.

69) China is the largest country with only one time zone; geographically, it has five time zones, but it chooses to use one standard time.

70) With two exceptions, China owns all the world's giant pandas. Any panda in a foreign zoo is on loan from China with the agreement that China owns the panda and any offspring; all offspring must also be returned to China before they are four years old. The only exceptions are two pandas China gave to Mexico before implementing the current policy.

71) With an annual average temperature of 85.8 degrees Fahrenheit, Khartoum, Sudan, is the world's hottest national capital city.

72) In 1891, Whitcomb Judson invented the zipper; it was originally for fastening shoes.

73) Women spend about one year of their lives deciding what to wear.

74) Unwinding a roll of Scotch tape can produce enough x-rays to image a finger. As the tape is unpeeled and its adhesive snaps free of the surface, flows of electrons are released. The electrical currents generate strong, short bursts of x-rays, each about one billionth of a second long and containing about 300,000 x-ray photons. Scientists were able to use the x-rays to image a finger. However, the phenomenon has been observed only when the tape is unpeeled in a vacuum.

75) The male antechinus, a small mouse-like mammal in Australia, essentially kills itself mating. During their first mating season, males mate as much as 14 hours straight with as many females as they can over three weeks. Physically, males rapidly deteriorate during the mating period, and very few survive.

76) Most of the world's supply of cork comes from cork oak trees, predominantly in Portugal and Spain.

77) Squidgers are the larger discs used to shoot the winks in tiddlywinks.

78) The frisbee was originally called the Pluto Platter.

79) Pumice is the only rock that floats in water.

80) In Victorian times, photography subjects were encouraged to say prunes instead of cheese. Among other reasons, Victorians thought it was classless to show a big toothy smile.

81) The spire on the Empire State building was meant to be used as an airship dock.

82) The United Kingdom and Great Britain are not the same. Great Britain includes England, Scotland, and Wales; the United Kingdom also includes Northern Ireland.

83) Mexican War hero Zachary Taylor was the first U.S president with no prior political experience.

84) At 0.05 millimeters thick, the eyelid is the thinnest skin on the human body; the palms and soles of the feet are the thickest, about 30 times thicker.

85) The boa constrictor is the only living animal that has the same common and scientific name.

86) A group of rhinoceros is called a crash.

87) On average, a person will die from a complete lack of sleep faster than from starvation. You can live about 11 days without sleep, but you can live weeks without food.

88) A normal house cat has 18 claws; there are five on each front paw and four on each back paw.

89) Genghis Khan once ordered his army to eat every tenth man. In 1214, Khan laid siege to the city of Chengdu, the capital of the Chinese Jin empire. The siege went on for a long time, and supplies were short; they were also ravaged by the plague. Khan ordered that every tenth man be sacrificed to feed the others. Khan personally abandoned the siege, leaving it to one of his generals, and Chengdu eventually fell in 1215.

90) The king rat can go longer without drinking than any other land animal; they can go their entire life, three to five years, without drinking.

91) Q-tips were originally called Baby Gays. They were originally for babies' eyes, ears, nostrils, and gums; the Q stands for quality.

92) Lethologica is the word for when you can't remember a word.

93) In Colombia and other South American countries, movie theaters sell spicy roasted ants that are munched the way Americans enjoy popcorn.

94) The word scientist was first used in 1833.

95) Due to spinal decompression, you are about one centimeter taller when you wake up in the morning.

96) Tim Berners-Lee, the inventor of the World Wide Web, regrets putting double slashes in URLs. It was a programming convention at the time, but it wasn't necessary and has caused a lot of wasted time typing and wasted paper printing.

97) The name Arctic is from the Greek word "Arktos," meaning bear; in this case, bear is a celestial reference to the Little and Great Bear constellations of the Northern Hemisphere. Antarctica comes from the Greek "Antarktikos," which means the opposite, and therefore, the opposite end of the earth.

98) Lesotho is the only country that lies completely above 1,000 meters elevation; it has an area of 11,720 square miles.

99) Insects don't flap their wings. An insect's wings are attached to its exoskeleton; they contract their muscles and force their whole body to vibrate, causing their wings to vibrate.

100) A strawberry isn't a berry, but a banana is. Botanically, a berry must have three layers: a protective outer layer, a fleshy middle, and an inner part that holds the seeds. It must also have two or more seeds and come from a flower with only one ovary. Strawberries come from a single flower with more than one ovary, making them an aggregate fruit.

101) Ravens, crows, jays, and some songbirds lie in anthills and roll around letting the ants swarm on them, or they chew up the ants and rub them on their feathers. It is called anting, and it isn't understood why they do it.

102) There are more insects in one square mile of empty field than there are people in the world.

103) The slime mold physarum polycephalum is neither a plant, an animal, nor a fungus, and it doesn't have two sexes; it has 720. It can also split into different organisms and fuse back together. It is bright yellow and can creep along at a speed of up to 1.6 inches per hour. It can also solve problems, even though it doesn't have a brain. The unicellular being is believed to be about a billion years old, but it first came to the public's attention in May 1973 after a Texas woman discovered a rapidly expanding yellow blob growing in her backyard. Researchers have found that physarum polycephalum can learn to ignore noxious substances and remember that behavior up to a year later. The slime mold is also believed to be capable of solving problems, such as finding the shortest way through a maze and anticipating changes in its environment. It lives on forest floors and thrives in temperatures between 66 and 77 degrees Fahrenheit and humidity levels between 80% and 100%. It is almost immortal; it can be killed by light and drought, but it can hibernate for several years when threatened.

104) The earliest pillows date back 9,000 years to Mesopotamia; they were made from stone, with a curved top, and were designed to keep the head off the ground and prevent insects from crawling into the mouth, nose, and ears.

105) Almost 3% of the ice in the Antarctic glaciers is from penguin urine.

106) Some people who get bitten by the lone star tick can develop a sudden allergy to red meat. The allergy affects the sensitivity to a carbohydrate called galactose-alpha-1,3-galactose, which is in most mammal cell membranes, so the allergy doesn't extend to poultry or seafood. The lone star tick has been recorded as far north as Maine and as far west as central Texas and Oklahoma.

107) Writing punctuation as we largely know it today did not exist until the 15th century.

108) You can fire a gun in the oxygen-free environment of space. Fires can't burn without oxygen, but modern ammunition contains its own oxidizer to trigger the explosion of gunpowder and fire the bullet; no atmospheric oxygen is required.

109) The nursery rhyme *Mary Had a Little Lamb* is based on the true story of Mary Sawyer of Sterling, Massachusetts, who as an 11-year-old was followed to school by her pet lamb. John Roulstone, a student a year or two older, handed Mary a piece of paper the next day with a poem he had written about it. In 1830, Sarah Josepha Hale, a well-known writer and editor, published *Poems for Our Children* that included a version of the poem.

110) Due to erosion, Niagara Falls has receded about seven miles over the last 12,500 years.

111) After going deaf, Beethoven discovered that he could bite on a metal pole connected to the piano he was playing and hear almost perfectly. This process is known as bone conduction; vibrations are transferred into the bones, and the ears pick up the signal with no sound distortion, bypassing the eardrums. We all hear sounds through both our bones and our eardrums; most sounds are air conducted, where the eardrum converts sound waves to vibrations and transmits them to the inner ear. In some cases, vibrations are heard directly by the inner ear, bypassing your eardrums. This is one of the ways you hear your own voice.

112) Of all paragraphs written in English, 80% contain the word "the."

113) The Japanese Onagadori chicken has the world's longest feathers; its tail feathers can measure over 10 meters.

114) Australia has the world's longest fence; the dingo fence was completed in 1885 and is 3,488 miles long.

115) Since it is exposed to the sun a lot of the time while they eat, a giraffe's tongue is black or purple to prevent sunburn.

116) From a standing position, pigs are physically incapable of looking up towards the sky.

117) South Africa is the first nation that created nuclear weapons and then voluntarily got rid of them.

118) As much as 95% of all dreams are forgotten shortly after waking. Research suggests that the changes in the brain during sleep do not support the information processing and storage for forming long-lasting memories.

119) The shortest country names have four letters: Chad, Togo, Mali, Iraq, Iran, Oman, Laos, Niue, Fiji, Cuba, and Peru.

120) If the earth's history was condensed to 24 hours, humans would appear at 11:58:43 p.m.

121) After the fall of the Roman Empire, the technology to make concrete was lost for 1,000 years. Roman concrete is still more durable than the concrete we make today, and it gets stronger over time. Their concrete was created with volcanic ash, lime, and seawater mixed with volcanic rock; it created a rock-like concrete we haven't been able to duplicate.

122) Mongolia is the least densely populated country; areas like Greenland have even lower density but aren't independent countries.

123) The 3 Musketeers candy bar got its name because it originally came in a package that had three pieces with different nougat flavors: vanilla, chocolate, and strawberry.

124) With less than 400 residents, Ngerulmud, Palau, is the world's smallest population national capital. Palau is an island nation in the Pacific Ocean.

125) Humans have a gaze detection system that is especially sensitive to whether someone is looking directly at you or whether their gaze is averted just a few degrees. Studies have recorded brain activity and found that specific brain cells fire when the gaze is direct; others fire if the gaze is just a few degrees off. Our brain specialization is an indication of how important eye contact is when communicating with others

126) Camel milk won't curdle. The structure of the protein in camel milk differs from cows, goats, sheep, and other animals; due to its composition, camel milk does not curdle naturally.

127) In ancient Egypt, the penalty for killing a cat, even accidentally, was death.

128) At normal atmospheric pressure, helium is the only element in the universe that can't freeze; it can't get cold enough.

129) At 19,341 feet, Mount Kilimanjaro is the world's highest mountain that isn't part of a range.

130) In England during WWI, people started wearing pajamas instead of nightgowns, so they would be prepared to run outside in public during air raids.

131) The blue whale is the largest animal that has ever lived. They can be up to 100 feet long and weigh 200 tons.

132) In 1863, a military draft was started to provide troops for the Union army during the American Civil War. The draft was set up to allow two ways that you could avoid going; you could pay $300 or find someone else to go in your place. What happened is that people paid $300 to have someone else go in their place. Some people made a career out of taking the money to be a substitute, deserting, and repeating the process.

133) In the 3rd century BC, Aristarchus of Samos first proposed that the planets orbited the sun. Copernicus developed a fully predictive model in the 16th century, but he wasn't the first to propose the concept.

134) The Indonesian word for water is air.

135) In the Braille system, there are six dots in each letter.

136) Arachibutyrophobia is the fear of peanut butter sticking to the roof of your mouth.

137) Koalas are one of the world's sleepiest animals; they sleep 22 hours per day.

138) By area, Manitoulin Island, in Lake Huron, is the world's largest freshwater island; it is over 1,000 square miles and is part of Ontario, Canada.

139) Marie Curie (1903 Physics and 1911 Chemistry) and Linus Pauling (1954 Chemistry and 1962 Peace) are the only people to win Nobel Prizes in two different categories.

140) In 1958 as part of a high school history class project, Robert Heft designed the current 50-star U.S. flag.

141) The onion is the world's most widely used vegetable.

142) Velociraptors were nothing like they were portrayed in the movie *Jurassic Park*. They were about 3 feet tall and 6 feet long including their tail; they had feathers and weighed about 30 pounds, the size of a large turkey.

143) Cleopatra was born 2,500 years after the Great Pyramid of Giza was built; she was closer to our current time than she was to the pyramids.

144) There are at least 24 dialects of English spoken in the United States.

145) Melanistic animals are the opposite of albinos. They are all black and have an excess of melanin that makes their skin, hair, or fur very dark or black.

146) Violet Jessop (1887–1971) survived the collision of the *RMS Olympic* on September 20, 1911, the sinking of the *RMS Titanic* on April 14, 1912, and the sinking of the *HMHS Britannic* on November 21, 1916. She was an ocean line stewardess and nurse.

147) In medieval manuscripts, it is common to see pictures of knights fighting snails; no one knows why.

148) The skin on a whale shark's back can be up to four inches thick, and they can make it even tougher by clenching the muscles just beneath their skin. Their underbellies are relatively soft and vulnerable, so they will often turn their belly away when approached.

149) As a defense mechanism, bombardier beetles emit a hot noxious chemical spray that is produced from a reaction between hydroquinone and hydrogen peroxide, which are stored in two reservoirs in the beetle's abdomen. When the solutions are mixed with catalysts, the heat from the reaction brings the mixture to near the boiling point of water and produces gas that drives the ejection. The spray can be fatal to attacking insects. There are over 500 species of bombardier beetles, and they live on all continents except Antarctica.

150) The Great Pyramid of Giza was originally covered in highly-polished white limestone; it was removed over time, so it could be used for other building projects.

151) On a clear night in a dark area, you can see about 2,000 stars in the sky.

152) On average, female anaconda snakes are 4.7 times larger than males; that is the largest size difference between sexes of any land vertebrate.

153) Scatomancy, the practice of telling the future through someone's poop, was popular in ancient Egypt.

154) Measured by its share of the world's population, the largest empire in history was the Persian Empire; in 480 BC, it accounted for approximately 44% of the world's population. Comparatively, the British Empire accounted for about 23% of the world's population at its peak.

155) WWI greatly increased the number of women wearing bras. Before the war, corsets were still the norm, but corset frames were mostly made of metal that was needed for the war effort, so in 1917, the U.S. War Industries Board asked American women to stop buying them, accelerating the move to bras.

156) Horseshoe crab blood is worth $14,000 per quart because its unique chemical properties make it very valuable for bacterial testing. It can coagulate around as little as one part in a trillion of bacterial contamination, and the reaction only takes 45 minutes, instead of two days with mammalian blood.

157) The giant clam is the largest mollusk and can reach 4 feet in length and weigh more than 500 pounds. They live in the warm waters of the South Pacific and Indian Oceans and can live more than 100 years.

158) The Pacific Ocean is so large that at some points it is antipodal to itself. Two points are antipodal if they are on diametrically opposite sides of the earth. At some points in the Pacific Ocean, you could go straight through the center of the earth and come out on the other side and still be in the Pacific Ocean.

159) The international distress signal one level less serious than Mayday is Pan-Pan; Securite is the third level.

160) By area, New Mexico is 0.2% water, the lowest percentage of any state.

161) Franklin D. Roosevelt was put on the dime primarily for his work for March of Dimes, which was originally called the National Foundation for Infantile Paralysis.

162) Sharks don't get cavities because the outside of their teeth is made of fluoride.

163) In the song "Yankee Doodle," the term macaroni means fashionable. In late 18th century England, the term macaroni came to mean stylish; in the song, it is used to mock the Americans, who think they can be stylish by simply sticking a feather in their cap.

164) Malaria is believed to have killed more people than any other disease in history; it still kills about 1 million people annually.

165) Thirty-five percent of the world's population drives on the left side.

166) More than 90% of your serotonin, the neurotransmitter that contributes to feelings of well-being and happiness, is produced in the digestive tract.

167) *Ben-Hur: A Tale of the Christ* was the first fictional novel blessed by the pope.

168) Including U.S. territories, the greatest distance between any two points in the United States is between Guam and the U.S. Virgin Islands; it is 9,514 miles from Point Udall, Guam, to Point Udall, St. Croix, U.S. Virgin Islands.

169) Ambisinistrous means no good with either hand; it is the opposite of ambidextrous.

170) Dragonflies may have the best vision of any animal. Humans have three light-sensitive proteins in the eye for red, blue, and green (tri-chromatic vision); dragonflies have up to 33. Their bulbous eyes have 30,000 facets and can see in all directions at once.

171) About 85% of humans only breathe out of one nostril at a time. They switch between nostrils about every four hours, although it varies by person, body position, and other factors.

172) A blue whale's arteries are so large that an adult human could swim through them.

173) Idaho was the last state explored by Europeans or Americans (not Native Americans); it wasn't explored until Lewis and Clark entered Idaho in 1805.

174) Opossums don't play dead. If frightened, they go into shock, which induces a comatose state that can last from 40 minutes to 4 hours.

175) The word goodbye is a contraction of "God be with ye."

176) The concept of giving a key to the city comes from medieval times when walled cities were locked at night, but someone with the key could come and go as they liked.

177) If you have bloodshot eyes after swimming in a pool, it isn't chlorine causing the reaction; it is urine mixing with the pool's chemicals. The nitrogen in urine combines with the chlorine and forms chloramine, causing eye irritation.

178) In the 19th century, Notre Dame Cathedral was almost demolished, but it was saved by Victor Hugo's *The Hunchback of Notre Dame*. Hugo wrote the novel partially to save the cathedral from demolition.

179) Different cells in the human body have very different lifespans. Sperm cells have a lifespan of about 3 days; colon cells die after about 4 days; white blood cells live for about 13 days; cells in the top layer of your skin live about 30 days. Red blood cells live for about 120 days; liver cells live about 18 months, and brain cells typically last an entire lifetime.

180) The practice of quarantine began during the 14th century when ships arriving in Venice from plague-infected ports were required to sit at anchor for 40 days before landing. The word quarantine derives from the Italian "quaranta giorni," which means 40 days.

181) In 1893, New Zealand was the first country to allow women to vote.

182) Queen Elizabeth II is the world's largest landowner; she technically owns 6.6 billion acres, about one-sixth of the world's land, including Canada and Australia.

183) Nepetalactone, the essential oil in catnip that gives the plant its characteristic odor, is about 10 times more effective at repelling mosquitoes than DEET, the compound found in most commercial insect repellents.

184) Cats don't have very good close vision, so when they are near water, they may not be able to see the water or the water level. That is why they will frequently paw the water to feel the level or move the dish to cause a disturbance in the water, so they can see it.

185) *All in the Family, The Golden Girls, Will & Grace,* and *Schitt's Creek* are the only four television series that won Emmys for all their main cast members.

186) The world's largest recorded turtle was a leatherback turtle that washed up on Harlech Beach, Wales, in 1988. It was estimated to be 100 years old and was almost 9 feet long and weighed 2,016 pounds.

187) Pen caps have a hole in them to minimize the risk of children inhaling them and choking to death. It is an international safety standard.

188) Founded in 1565, St. Augustine, Florida, is the oldest U.S. city.

189) Hawaii is the only state without a straight line in its border; its borders are entirely defined by natural features.

190) There are 60 seconds in a minute and 360 degrees in a circle because the ancient Babylonians did math in base 60 instead of base 10 and developed the concepts.

191) Chang is the world's most common surname.

192) To avoid dating relatives, Iceland has a phone app that lets users bump phones to see if they are related. Iceland has a relatively small population of over 300,000 people and is somewhat insular, so most people are distantly related. The app emits a warning alarm if people are closely related, so they know not to date.

193) You can never recall a single memory by itself; memories are always recalled in packages because that is how the hippocampus stores them.

194) Excluding man, dolphins have the longest tested memory. Bottlenose dolphins have unique whistles, like names; studies have shown that they remember the whistle of other dolphins they have lived with, even after 20 years of separation.

195) Humans need 16 to 20 images per second to perceive something as a moving picture, rather than a flickering image; dogs need 70 images per second. Older televisions could only produce 50 images per second, so dogs would only see flickering images. Modern televisions are fast enough to appear as moving pictures to dogs.

196) The left leg of a chicken is more tender than the right. Chickens scratch with their right leg, building up more muscle in that leg and making it tougher than the left.

197) A group of butterflies is called a kaleidoscope.

198) A Japanese men's marathon runner at the 1912 Stockholm Olympics ended up with an official finishing time of 54 years, 8 months, 6 days, 5 hours, 32 minutes, and 20.3 seconds. When he went to the Stockholm games, Shizo Kanakuri was an experienced runner and held the 25-mile world record; he started the race, but temperatures of almost 90 degrees Fahrenheit forced him to drop out after more than 18 miles. He did not notify the officials, and feeling ashamed that he did not finish, he went quietly back to Japan and was listed as missing in the results. In 1967, a Swedish television show started looking for the missing marathon runner, and at the age of 75, Kanakuri was invited to Sweden for the 55th anniversary of the 1912 games. He was allowed to finish the race and receive an official time.

199) Iceland has the highest per capita electricity consumption; it is about four times higher than the United States.

200) In 1989, the first website was launched by CERN.

201) In ancient Egypt, men sat to pee and women stood.

202) Alcatraz used to be the only U.S. federal prison where inmates got hot showers. They didn't want inmates to get acclimatized to cold water, in case they tried to swim to shore.

203) Winnie the Pooh's real name is Edward Bear.

204) Forty percent of schizophrenics are left-handed; only 10% of the total population is left-handed.

205) Wilmer McLean's homes were involved in both the beginning and end of the American Civil War. On July 21, 1861, the First Battle of Bull Run took place on his farm near Manassas, Virginia. To escape the war, he moved to Appomattox, Virginia, but in 1865, General Robert E. Lee surrendered to Ulysses S. Grant in McLean's house in Appomattox.

206) Twenty-two countries don't maintain an army, including Andorra, Costa Rica, Panama, Grenada, Haiti, Iceland, and Liechtenstein.

207) Suriname has a higher percentage of forested land than any other country.

208) The Articles of Confederation, the original constitution of the United States, included an open invitation for Canada to join the United States. Ratified in 1781, they were replaced by the U.S. Constitution in 1789. If it wanted to join the United States, there was a clause stating Canada would automatically be accepted without the consent of the other states.

209) With the dissolution of the Soviet Union, 15 independent republics were created: Russia, Ukraine, Georgia, Belarus, Uzbekistan, Armenia, Azerbaijan, Kazakhstan, Kyrgyzstan, Moldova, Turkmenistan, Tajikistan, Latvia, Lithuania, and Estonia.

210) Sacagawea has more U.S. statues in her honor than anyone else.

211) Wallace's giant bee is the world's largest bee species; it is native to Indonesia and was thought to be extinct for over a century until it was rediscovered in 1981. Females have a 2.5-inch wingspan and are about 1.5 inches long.

212) Fruit flies produce the largest sperm of any animal. Their sperm is coiled up and unspools to about 2.3 inches, approximately 20 times the length of their body and 1,000 times larger than human sperm.

213) In 2013, the remains of England's King Richard III were found buried under a parking lot in Leicester England; in 1485, he was the last English king to die on the battlefield.

214) Alaska receives the least sunshine of any state.

215) Lake Nicaragua is one of the world's very few freshwater lakes with sharks. Bull sharks can survive in both fresh and salt water, and they make their way back and forth from the Caribbean Sea to Lake Nicaragua via a 120-mile route through the San Juan River. Researchers have tagged sharks and verified that they move back and forth between the lake and the sea.

216) There is a basketball court one floor above the U.S. Supreme Court. It is called "The Highest Court in the Land" and was once a spare room to house journals. In the 1940s, it was converted into a workout area for courthouse workers, and backboards and baskets were installed later. It is smaller than a regulation basketball court and is used by clerks, off-duty police officers, and other supreme court employees.

217) Canada is the only country where more than 50% of its adults have college degrees.

218) People have surfed for 8 miles and over 30 minutes continuously riding a wave upstream on the Amazon River. The Pororoca is a tidal bore wave that is up to 13 feet high, travels up to 500 miles inland upstream, and has become popular with surfers. The wave occurs during new and full moons when the ocean tide is the highest and water flows in from the Atlantic. The phenomenon is most pronounced during the spring equinox in March when the moon and the sun are in direct alignment with the earth, and their gravitational pull is combined. The wave can be quite destructive as it moves upriver, and the water is filled with debris.

219) The 1666 Great Fire of London burned for five days and destroyed almost 90% of London's homes, but it only killed eight people.

220) Penguins can swim faster because they have a bubble boost; they fluff their feathers and release bubbles that reduce the density of the water around them. The bubbles act as lubrication that decreases water viscosity.

221) Memories continually change. They are malleable and are reconstructed with each recall; what we remember changes each time we recall the event. The slightly changed memory becomes the current memory, only to be reconstructed with the next recall.

222) George Washington's salary as U.S. president was $25,000. Based on the change in the consumer price index, it would equate to over $700,000 in today's dollars; today's presidential salary is $400,000.

223) Completed in 1885, the world's first skyscraper was Chicago's Home Insurance Building. It was 10 stories and 136 feet tall and was demolished in 1931.

224) Napoleon wasn't short for his time. He was about 5'7"; the average adult French male of his time was only 5'5", so he was taller than average. Some of the confusion is the units his height was reported in, and his guards, who he was usually seen with, were required to be quite tall.

225) Instead of the normal five senses, neuroscientists define somewhere between 22-33 different senses known as meta-senses. Some of the common meta-senses are equilibrioception (your sense of balance), proprioception (knowing which parts of your body are where without looking), and thermoception (being able to sense temperature).

226) Eight people took refuge on Noah's ark, Noah and his wife and his three sons and their wives.

227) Lobsters have urine release nozzles right under their eyes, and they urinate as a way of communicating with each other.

228) Iceland has the world's oldest parliament; it has existed since 930 AD.

229) Yellowstone National Park has most of the world's geysers.

230) The hard piece at the end of a shoelace is called an aglet.

231) America's first bank robbery occurred in August 1798 at the Bank of Pennsylvania in Philadelphia. The robbers got away with $162,821, and it resulted in a false imprisonment trial, a book, and the real robber depositing some of the stolen money back in the bank. Blacksmith Patrick Lyon became the primary suspect because he had recently installed new locks on the vault doors of the bank; he was arrested and eventually convicted. However, the real robbers were Thomas Cunningham and Isaac Davis. Cunningham was a porter at the bank and the inside man; he died of yellow fever soon after the robbery. Davis was caught after depositing stolen money at banks around Philadelphia, including the bank he robbed. However, he was given a pardon for making a full confession and returning the money; he never spent any time in jail. Lyon served three months in prison before being released; he wrote a book about his experience and sued for wrongful imprisonment. It was one of the first trials in the U.S. dealing with the concept of probable cause, and he won $12,000 in damages.

232) On average over their lifetime, a person grows 450 miles of hair on their head.

233) The company Google was originally called Backrub.

234) Pablo Picasso's work is stolen more than any other painter.

235) Thirty-two countries use the dollar (either the U.S. dollar or other dollar) as their official currency: Australia, Bahamas, Barbados, Belize, Brunei, Canada, Dominica, East Timor, Ecuador, El Salvador, Fiji, Grenada, Guyana, Jamaica, Kiribati, Liberia, Marshall Islands, Micronesia, Namibia, Nauru, New Zealand, Palau, Saint Kitts and Nevis, Saint Lucia, Saint Vincent and the Grenadines, Singapore, Solomon Islands, Suriname, Taiwan, Tuvalu, United States, and Zimbabwe.

236) Outer space smells most like the burning odor of hydrocarbons; astronauts have reported smelling burned or fried steak after a spacewalk.

237) There were eight U.S. national capital cities before Washington, D.C.: Philadelphia, Pennsylvania; Baltimore, Maryland; Lancaster Pennsylvania; York, Pennsylvania; Princeton, New Jersey; Annapolis, Maryland; Trenton, New Jersey; and New York City, New York.

238) Greece invented cheesecake.

239) Sea otters have the densest fur of all animals; they have up to one million hairs per square inch on the densest parts of their body.

240) A group of pandas is called an embarrassment.

241) Lebanon is the only Middle Eastern country without a desert.

242) U.S. television allows alcohol to be advertised if no alcohol is consumed in the commercial; it isn't a law or FCC regulation, just a broadcasting standard.

243) Pirates wore earrings to improve their eyesight; they believed the precious metals in an earring had healing powers.

244) To absorb urine and feces, both male and female astronauts wear a maximum absorbency garment, an adult diaper with extra absorption material, during liftoff, landing, and extra-vehicular activity. These operations can take a long time or have significant delays, and astronauts can't just get up and go to the bathroom at any time.

245) Annapolis, Maryland, and Albany, New York, are the only two state capitals named for royalty. Annapolis is named for Princess Anne of Denmark and Norway, who became Queen of England; Albany is named for the Duke of York and Albany, who became King James II of England.

246) Sand dunes cover only about 15% of the Sahara Desert; rock plateaus and coarse gravel cover the majority.

247) Kinderschema is a set of physical characteristics that humans are naturally drawn toward; the characteristics include a rounded belly, big head, big eyes, loose limbs, etc. Puppies, kittens, and other animals, including human babies, trigger kinderschema. Humans have an intrinsic motivation to care for babies and children; these tendencies have developed through millions of years of evolution.

248) With an estimated 500 million copies sold, *Don Quixote* is the best-selling fiction book of all time; *A Tale of Two Cities* is second at about 200 million copies.

249) Less than 1% of bacteria cause disease in humans.

250) The lens of the eye continues to grow throughout a person's life.

251) The Caspian Sea is the world's largest enclosed inland body of water; it is considered a lake by some, but it has salt water. It has 3.5 times more water than all the Great Lakes combined.

252) The footprints left behind by astronauts on the moon could last 10 to 100 million years. The moon has no atmosphere, so there is no wind or water to blow or wash anything away.

253) Human embryos develop fingerprints three months after conception.

254) Snail slime is mucus that lubricates the surface and helps them move faster with less friction; they often travel in the mucus trails of other snails to move faster.

255) September's name comes from the Latin "septem," meaning seven. It was the seventh month in the old Roman calendar, where the year started with March; its name was carried over to the Julian and current Gregorian calendars, where it is the ninth month.

256) When poured, hot water has a higher pitch than cold water. Water changes viscosity with temperature, which affects the sound when poured.

257) William Shakespeare's *Henry IV, Part 1* is responsible for starlings being introduced to North America. Eugene Schieffelin, chairman of the American Acclimatization Society, wanted to import every bird mentioned in Shakespeare's works, and the starling is only mentioned in *Henry IV, Part 1*. In 1890, he released starlings in New York's Central Park.

258) Sulfur gives onions their distinctive smell; when cut or crushed, a chemical reaction changes an amino acid into a sulfur compound.

259) On December 28th, 1973, the first mutiny in space occurred on *Skylab 4*. The three-man crew turned off radio communications with NASA for a full day and spent the day relaxing. They had already spent as much time in space as anyone ever had and were tired of the demanding schedule NASA had set for them. After the day off, they continued their duties and spent about another month in space, setting the record at the time of 84 days.

260) Aluminum is the major constituent of rubies.

261) Europe is the only continent without a significant desert.

262) Snails slide around on a single foot; the one long muscle acts like a human extremity and helps them grip and push themselves along the ground.

263) The first chocolate treat was hot chocolate during the Aztec civilization.

264) The elephant probably spends more time standing than any other mammal. In the wild, they live up to 70 years, and they only sleep about two hours a day. They also often sleep standing up, only lying down every few nights.

265) Humans make up about 0.01% of the earth's biomass; plants account for about 80%; bacteria account for 13%, and fungi are 2%. In total, animals account for about 0.36%, with insects making up about half of that and fish accounting for another third.

266) Mr. and Mrs. are abbreviations for master and mistress.

267) In the 1600s, some doctors recommended their patients fart into jars and store them to later inhale to ward off the bubonic plague. The idea was that the plague was caused by deadly vapors, so it could be warded off by foul vapors.

268) The Australian continent has an average elevation of 1,083 feet, the lowest of any continent.

269) Bhutan's Gangkhar Puensum is the world's highest unclimbed mountain. It is 24,840 feet high and has been off-limits to climbers since 1994 when Bhutan prohibited all mountaineering above 6,000 meters due to spiritual and religious beliefs.

270) Sideburns are named after American Civil War general Ambrose Burnside; he was known for having an unusual facial hairstyle with a mustache connected to thick sideburns and a clean-shaven chin.

271) The gender of most turtles, alligators, and crocodiles is determined after fertilization. The temperature of the eggs decides whether the offspring will be male or female; this is called temperature-dependent sex determination.

272) Without an air circulation system, a flame in zero gravity, even in a pure oxygen environment, will extinguish itself. A typical flame produces light, heat, carbon dioxide, and water vapor; the heat causes the combustion products to expand, lowering their density, and they rise, allowing fresh, oxygen-containing air to get to the flame. In zero gravity, neither buoyancy nor convection occurs; therefore, the combustion products accumulate around the flame, preventing oxygen from reaching it, and the flame goes out.

273) A galactic or cosmic year is the amount of time it takes the sun to orbit once around the center of the Milky Way Galaxy, about 230 million years.

274) Beetles are the most common type of insect eaten by humans.

275) The Bible doesn't say Adam and Eve ate an apple. It says they ate the forbidden fruit from the tree of knowledge; nowhere does it say it was an apple.

276) Inspired by burrs, George de Mestral invented Velcro in the 1940s.

277) If you started with $0.01 and had a 100% daily return on your money, you would be a millionaire in 27 days.

278) A female octopus can lay tens of thousands of eggs at one time, and when they hatch, she dies. She reproduces only once, and after she lays her eggs, she doesn't eat and puts all her energy into caring for them.

279) In WWII, Tootsie Rolls were part of soldier rations; they were durable in all weather conditions and were good for quick energy.

280) If the moon didn't exist, a day on Earth would be 6-8 hours long.

281) The average pencil has enough graphite to draw a line 35 miles long or write about 45,000 words.

282) Against explicit orders, Portuguese diplomat Aristides de Sousa Mendes issued an estimated 30,000 Portuguese travel visas for Jewish families fleeing Nazi persecution. He was stripped of his diplomatic position and forbidden from earning a living, and his 15 children were also blacklisted and prevented from attending university or finding meaningful work. He died in 1954, and the first recognition of his heroism didn't come until 1966 when Israel declared him to be a "Righteous Among the Nations." In 1986, the U.S. Congress also issued a proclamation honoring his heroic act.

283) The greatest distance on the earth between the nearest points of land is 994 miles from Bouvet Island in the South Atlantic to Antarctica.

284) During the American Civil War, women were prohibited from enlisting in both the Union and Confederate armies, but dressed as men, more than 600 women joined the war anyway.

285) German chocolate cake originated in the United States; it was named after American baker Samuel German.

286) Currently, an Olympic gold medal is 92.5% silver.

287) The first recorded worker's strike took place in ancient Egypt in 1152 BC when the artisans of the Royal Necropolis at Deir el-Medina organized an uprising. It took place under the rule of Pharaoh Ramses III and was recorded on papyrus.

288) Alaska has all five of the largest land area cities in the United States: Yakutat, Sitka, Juneau, Wrangell, and Anchorage.

289) Prairie dogs greet each other by kissing; the kiss involves touching their teeth together to determine whether the prairie dog they are greeting is a member of their social group.

290) The cutaneous marginal pouch, informally known as Henry's pocket, is the fold of skin forming an open pouch at the outer base of a cat's ear. Some dogs also have it.

291) Jack Swigert originally said, "Houston, we've had a problem here." The quote is sometimes incorrectly attributed to James Lovell, who repeated, "Houston, we've had a problem," and it is not "Houston, we have a problem," as depicted in the movie.

292) Instead of the five tastes (sweet, savory, sour, bitter, and salty) that humans can detect, whales and dolphins can only taste salty.

293) President John Quincy Adams received a pet alligator as a gift and kept it in the White House East Room bathroom for two months before returning it.

294) Damascus, Syria, is widely regarded as the world's oldest continuously inhabited city; it has been inhabited for at least 11,000 years.

295) Humans swallow on average twice a minute, even while sleeping.

296) The tufts of hair in a cat's ear are called ear furnishings; they help keep out dirt, direct sounds, and insulate the ears.

297) In Guinea, wild chimpanzees drink fermented palm sap that contains up to 6.9% alcohol. Some of the chimpanzees consume significant quantities and exhibit signs of inebriation.

298) In humans, the right lung is always larger than the left. The left lung is smaller to leave room for the heart.

299) Louis Bonaparte, Napoleon's brother, was called the "King of Rabbits" because he mispronounced the Dutch phrase "I am your King" and instead said, "I am your rabbit," when he took over rule of the Netherlands in 1806.

300) When they poop, dogs stare at you because they know they are vulnerable at that time, and they are looking to you, a member of their pack, for protection.

301) Clouds appear to be darker because they are thicker, which prevents more light from passing through; thinner clouds allow more light through and appear white. As seen from an airplane, the top of the cloud will still appear white since the top receives more light. As water droplets and ice crystals in a cloud thicken when it is about to rain, they scatter much less light, and the cloud appears almost black.

302) Mount Chimborazo, Ecuador, is closer to the moon than any other place on the earth. It is 20,548 feet in elevation, but it is very close to the equator, so the bulge in the earth makes it 1.5 miles closer to the moon than Mount Everest.

303) Rome, Italy, is located at about the same latitude as the southernmost point of Canada.

304) Sandwiches didn't appear in American cookbooks until 1815.

305) Early humans in South America hunted giant armadillos that were about the size and weight of a Volkswagen Beetle; they used their shells for homes.

306) The Greek national anthem "Hymn to Liberty" has 158 verses and is the longest national anthem in the world. It is an 1823 poem by Dionysios Solomos set to music by Nikolaos Mantzaros.

307) Your eardrums move when your eyes move; the reason is unclear.

308) The human eye has enough visual acuity that you could see a candle flame 30 miles away on a dark night if the earth were flat.

309) Researchers have found that most mammals weighing at least six pounds take about 21 seconds to urinate. The number seems quite consistent with the urethra scaled to deliver about the same time, regardless of the animal size.

310) In a show of dominance, male Indian rhinos can spray urine over 16 feet; this is typically done in the presence of other males or breeding-age females.

311) Thomas Jefferson did not like public speaking and preferred to remain quiet most of the time. He only made two speeches during his entire eight-year presidency; they were both inaugural speeches and were hardly audible.

312) Cats and humans have almost identical brain structures, including the region that controls emotion. Cats have temporal, occipital, frontal, and parietal lobes in their brains, just like humans, and the connections within their brains seem to mirror those of humans. Their brains also release neurotransmitters, and they have short and long-term memory.

313) At 19,714 feet deep, Tibet's Yarlung Tsangpo Canyon is the world's deepest canyon.

314) The Memphis, Tennessee, Bass Pro Shops Megastore is one of the world's largest pyramids and features a hotel, indoor swamp, aquarium, bowling alley, and the world's tallest freestanding elevator. The pyramid is 321 feet tall and has a 535,000 square foot interior.

315) The liver is the only human internal organ that can regenerate itself. You can lose up to 75% of your liver, and the remaining portion can regenerate into a whole liver. Therefore, living donor transplants where a portion of the liver is taken are possible; both the donor and recipient's portion regrows into a full liver within about four months. A liver from a deceased donor may also be split and transplanted into two recipients.

316) In 1958, Nils Bohlin, an engineer at Volvo, invented the revolutionary three-point seat belt used today; to save lives, Volvo gave away the patent for free.

317) Only once in history has a submerged submarine deliberately sunk a submerged submarine. In 1945, a British submarine sunk a German submarine.

318) Before 1938, toothbrushes were made using boar hairs.

319) The green sea slug, which lives off the east coast of the United States, is the first animal ever discovered that is also part plant. The slugs take chloroplasts into their skin, which turns it emerald green and makes it capable of photosynthesis. They can go without eating for nine months or more, photosynthesizing as they bask in the sun.

320) Adult dogs have 42 teeth; puppies have 28 baby teeth.

321) Dogs normally start sniffing with their right nostril and keep using the right nostril if the smell is something unpleasant or potentially dangerous. If the smell is something pleasant, they will switch to using their left nostril.

322) A Swedish mathematician calculated that there are 177,147 different ways to tie a necktie knot. The number accounts for variations in exposed knots, wrappings, and windings.

323) On December 21, 1913, the first published crossword puzzle appeared in the *New York World* newspaper.

324) The highest and lowest points in the contiguous United States are in the same county. Mount Whitney, at 14,494 feet, and Death Valley's Badwater Basin, at 282 feet below sea level, are separated by 85 miles in Inyo County, California.

325) In the last century, the east coast of the United States has moved about eight feet further away from Europe.

326) Four is the only number spelled out in English that has the same number of letters as its value.

327) Swans have 24 neck vertebrae, more than any other warm-blooded animal.

328) When written out in English, no number before one thousand contains the letter a.

329) Over 2,300 years ago, Hippocrates described walking as "man's best medicine."

330) In math, a lemniscate shape means infinity; lemniscate is the word for a shape with two loops meeting at a central point.

331) There are an estimated 1 million spiders per acre of land; in the tropics, there are closer to 3 million per acre.

332) Based on its global following, soccer is the world's most popular sport; cricket is second; field hockey is third.

333) If you ate a polar bear's liver, you would get vitamin A poisoning and could die. Polar bears have 50-60 times the normal human levels of vitamin A in their liver, about three times the tolerable level that a human can intake.

334) In total darkness, most people naturally adjust to a 48-hour cycle, instead of 24 hours. They have 36 hours of activity followed by 12 hours of sleep; the reasons are unclear.

335) The Easter Island statues have full bodies, not just heads. The remainder of the body is buried; the tallest statue excavated is 33 feet high.

336) Scientists have tracked Alpine swifts that can fly for 200 days straight without ever landing. They are a swallow-like bird found in Europe, Africa, and Asia, and they eat and sleep while flying and never leave the air.

337) More than 1 trillion photographs are taken annually; more photographs are taken every two minutes than were taken in total up through the 1800s.

338) Excluding eye injuries, pirates likely wore eye patches to see in the dark. They were constantly going above and below deck, and it takes the human eye up to 25 minutes to adapt to seeing in the dark. By wearing a patch, they kept one eye dark adjusted, so they could see in the dark immediately by moving the eye patch.

339) It takes about 90 minutes to hard boil an ostrich egg.

340) The Egyptian civilization was the first to divide the day into 24 hours. Ancient Egyptians used a base 12 system, instead of our base 10 system; they counted the knuckles of each finger, using their thumbs as pointers. They had 12 hours of light and 12 hours of darkness, so the length of the hours varied by time of the year. Fixed length hours were proposed by the Greeks in the 2nd century BC, but they did not become common until mechanical clocks first appeared in Europe during the 14th century.

341) New Zealand has a higher percentage of households with pets than any other country; about 68% of households have a pet.

342) Turritopsis dohrnii, also known as the immortal jellyfish, is essentially biologically immortal. Once the adult jellyfish have reproduced, they transform themselves back into their juvenile state. Their tentacles retract; their bodies shrink, and they sink to the ocean floor and start their life cycle all over again. They can do it repeatedly, making them essentially immortal unless they are consumed by another animal or struck by disease.

343) More people die of drowning in the desert than die of dehydration. Flash floods in desert areas kill more people than dehydration.

344) In 1678, Italian Elena Cornaro Piscopia was the world's first woman to receive a Ph.D. degree.

345) The longest period any sports trophy has been successfully defended is 132 years. America's Cup for sailing was held by the United States from its start in 1851 until Australia won in 1983.

346) The reminiscence bump is the tendency to have increased recollection of events that occurred during adolescence and early adulthood. The bump occurs from about 16 to 25 years of age. Memory storage is not consistent through time; it increases during times of change in self and life goals that typically happen during the reminiscence bump years.

347) Alien hand syndrome, sometimes called Dr. Strangelove syndrome, is a condition where a person's limb acts seemingly on its own without control. It can be caused by the separation of the brain hemispheres and most frequently affects the left hand.

348) From the 1830s to the 1930s, the collars on men's dress shirts were typically detachable; this was to save on laundry since the collar is the part that most frequently needs cleaning.

349) Submarines made their first wartime appearance during the American Revolutionary War. On September 6, 1776, *Turtle*, a submersible built by American David Bushnell, was used in an attempted attack on the British ship *Eagle*. It was a one-man wooden craft that relied on a human-powered hand crank and foot treadle for propulsion. A pedal-operated water tank allowed it to submerge and surface; lead ballast kept it upright in the water.

350) President Thomas Jefferson is commonly credited with inventing the swivel chair.

351) Taumatawhakatangihangakoauauotamateaturipukakapikimaun-gahoronukupokaiwhenuakitanatahu is the world's longest place name; it is a hill in New Zealand.

352) With speeds up to 242 mph including hunting dives, the peregrine falcon is the world's fastest bird.

353) At its triple point, a liquid can exist simultaneously as a liquid, solid, and gas. The triple point is the temperature and pressure that puts the three states of matter into a thermodynamic equilibrium, where no state is trying to change into any other state. The boiling liquid causes high-energy molecules to rise as a gas; this lowers the temperature of the boiling liquid and makes it freeze. The cycle continues if the triple point temperature and pressure are maintained. For water, the triple point is at 32.02 degrees Fahrenheit and 0.006 atmospheres (normal pressure is 1 atmosphere).

354) At its peak, the British Empire was the largest empire by area in history; in 1922, it ruled over about 24% of the world's land.

355) By slowing their heart rate, sloths can hold their breath for 40 minutes.

356) If a patient died during surgery in ancient Egypt, the surgeon's hands were cut off.

357) Of all the text information stored on the world's computers, 80% is in English.

358) The orangutan is the largest tree-dwelling animal. They are up to 4.5 feet tall, weigh up to 200 pounds, and spend nearly all their time in the forest canopy.

359) In 5 BC, Rome was the first city to reach a population of 1 million people.

360) Located in Fez, Morocco, the al-Qarawiyyin library is the world's oldest working library, operating since 859 AD.

361) Crapulous is the feeling you get from eating or drinking too much.

362) Everyone who has walked on the moon was born before 1936. Charles Duke, the tenth person to walk on the moon, was born the latest, October 3, 1935.

363) San Marino has the world's oldest surviving constitution; it dates to 1600. The U.S. constitution is the second oldest.

364) Leeches have 32 brains; each controls a different segment of their body.

365) Captain James Cook was the first man to set foot on all the continents other than Antarctica.

366) The Mexican free-tailed bat is the world's fastest mammal. It can reach speeds of 100 mph in normal flight.

367) The force required to topple a domino is less than the force it generates when it falls; this force amplification can be used to topple ever-larger dominos. Each domino can be about 1.5 times larger than the preceding one. Starting with a regular size domino at about 1.875 inches tall and pushing it over, the 25th domino toppled would be about 2,630 feet tall, about the height of the world's tallest building.

368) The banana is the world's largest herb plant, with species growing up to 100 feet tall; it doesn't have a true woody trunk like a tree and behaves like a perennial.

369) A poker hand with two black aces and two black eights is known as the "dead man's hand" because it is the hand Wild Bill Hickok was holding when he was killed.

370) Bananas, along with other potassium-rich foods like spinach, apricots, salmon, avocados, and mushrooms, are radioactive. K-40 radioactive atoms make up a very small fraction of potassium atoms; they spontaneously decay, releasing beta radiation and gamma rays that are both capable of tissue damage. However, with a half-life of 1.3 billion years, K-40 is not very radioactive, so you would have to eat about 10 million bananas to die of radiation poisoning.

371) Humans produce about 1.5 quarts of mucus per day and swallow most of it.

372) Ninety percent of all English written material is made up of just 1,000 words.

373) The Volkswagen Beetle was the first car model to sell 20 million units.

374) The columella nasi is the fleshy end of your nose that splits your nostrils.

375) The seahorse and pipefish are the only two species of fish where the male gives birth.

376) Research shows that all blue-eyed people may be related; they believe the trait comes from a single individual whose genes mutated between 6,000 and 10,000 years ago. Before that, everyone had varying shades of brown eyes.

377) The term "pixel" is short for picture element.

378) The logo of New Zealand's Royal Air Force is the kiwi, a flightless bird.

379) The common cold likely came from camels. Researchers have found that along with being the source of the Middle East Respiratory Syndrome (MERS) virus, camels are the likely source of the common cold that spread to humans thousands of years ago.

380) Indonesia has the most earthquakes of any country; Japan has the second most.

381) A giraffe has the highest blood pressure of any animal; it is about 300 over 200.

382) On April 10, 1996, Tropical Cyclone Olivia produced a 253-mph wind on Barrow Island, Australia, the world's highest surface wind speed ever recorded.

383) Despite deaths and injuries, staged train collisions were a spectator attraction from 1896 up until the Great Depression. In 1896, Crush, Texas, was a temporary site established for a one-day publicity stunt of a staged train wreck. It was organized by William George Crush, general passenger agent of the Missouri-Kansas-Texas Railroad. No admission was charged, but the railway charged $2 for every round-trip to get to the site, and there was a restaurant, midway, and medicine show. An estimated 40,000 people attended. For the main event, two unmanned six-car trains crashed into each other at 50 mph. Despite what mechanics had assured, the steam boilers on both trains exploded, creating flying debris that killed two people and injured many others. The spectators had been required to observe the collision from a hill 200 yards away, but they still weren't safe from the flying wood and metal. The staged collisions became popular, and Scott Joplin even wrote the "Great Crush Collision March."

384) At an elevation of 11,942 feet, La Paz, Bolivia, is the world's highest elevation national capital city.

385) Between 1530 and 1780, over 1 million Europeans were captured and sold as slaves to North Africa.

386) Orville Wright was the pilot in the first fatal airplane crash.

387) Alaska is both the westernmost and easternmost state; parts of Alaska stretch into the Eastern Hemisphere.

388) Crocodiles and alligators can climb trees. Researchers have found adults as high as 6 feet off the ground, and juveniles have been spotted as high as 30 feet.

389) Bird's nest soup is made from the nests of swifts; the nest is saliva that has dried and hardened.

390) A group of porcupines is called a prickle.

391) Michelangelo was struck in the face by a rival with a mallet and disfigured for life.

392) A college football game registered as an earthquake. The Earthquake Game was played between LSU and Auburn on October 8, 1988, at LSU's Tiger Stadium, with a crowd of 79,431 spectators. Auburn led 6-0 with less than two minutes left when LSU drove down the field and eventually threw an 11-yard touchdown pass on fourth down. The crowd's reaction to the touchdown pass registered as an earthquake on a seismograph located about 1,000 feet from the stadium at LSU's Howe-Russell Geoscience Complex. A seismologist noticed the reading the next day.

393) Arkansas has the only active diamond mine in the United States.

394) The term jaywalker originated because jay was a term for an idiot or simpleton and was often applied to rural people; therefore, jaywalking was being stupid, ignoring signs, and crossing the street in an unsafe place.

395) President Chester A. Arthur is regarded as the most fashionable U.S. president and owned 80 pairs of pants, which he liked to change several times a day.

396) Jane Austen referenced baseball over 40 years before it was invented. In 1797 in her novel *Northanger Abbey*, Austen wrote, "It was not very wonderful that Catherine, who had nothing heroic about her, should prefer cricket, base-ball, riding on horseback, and running about the country at the age of fourteen, to books." Baseball was supposedly invented by Abner Doubleday in Cooperstown, New York, in 1839; however, there are other earlier references to baseball in America. To avoid broken windows, a 1791 bylaw in Pittsfield, Massachusetts, banned the playing of "wicket, cricket, baseball, batball, football, cat, fives or any other game or games with balls" within 80 yards of the town meeting house. The name was certainly in use many decades before the current game was invented; the question is how much different the game was.

397) Due to a metal shortage during WWII, Oscars were made of painted plaster for three years. Following the war, the Academy invited recipients to trade in their plaster awards for gold-plated metal statuettes.

398) Marie Curie (1903 Physics and 1911 Chemistry) and her daughter Irene Juliot-Curie (1935 Chemistry) are the only mother and daughter to both win Nobel Prizes.

399) A mondegreen is a mishearing or misinterpretation of a phrase in a way that gives it a new meaning, such as when you mishear the lyrics of a song and insert words that sound similar and make sense.

400) Before 1859, baseball umpires used to sit in chairs behind home plate; they used rocking chairs that were 20 feet behind the batter.

401) The shortest complete English sentence is "Go."

402) Horses have weak ciliary muscles that do a poor job of focusing their eyes, so they need to move their heads to adjust the focal length or angle of view until the image falls into view on a portion of their retina.

403) The whale shark has the world's largest egg, up to 12 inches long; the ostrich has the largest laid egg.

404) Picasso used house paint in his paintings.

405) American microbiologist Maurice Ralph Hilleman (1919-2005) is credited with saving more lives than any other medical scientist of the 20th century. He specialized in developing vaccines and developed over 40 in his career, including 8 of the 14 vaccines routinely recommended: measles, mumps, hepatitis A, hepatitis B, chickenpox, meningitis, pneumonia, and Haemophilus influenzae.

406) Due to a shortage of space in London to bury people, the London Necropolis Railway line was opened in 1854 to carry corpses and mourners between London and the Brookwood Cemetery, 23 miles southwest of London. At the time, it was the world's largest cemetery and was designed to accommodate all London deaths for centuries. The station waiting rooms and the train compartments for both living and dead passengers were partitioned by religion and class to prevent mixing mourners and cadavers from different social backgrounds. By 1941, slightly over 200,000 burials had been conducted in the cemetery, which was far fewer than planned, and the railway line wasn't used again after being damaged during WWII.

407) Moray eels have two pairs of jaws. They have strong flesh-tearing primary jaws that can cut through bone, and they have a pharyngeal jaw, a second pair of jaws located in their throat. When the eel captures prey with its primary jaws, it can use its secondary pharyngeal jaws to grab the prey and drag it down into its gullet.

408) The famous Hollywood sign in Los Angeles originally said Hollywoodland. The sign was erected in 1923 as an advertisement for an upscale real estate development called Hollywoodland; in 1949, it was changed to its current form.

409) For every grain of sand on the earth, there are about 10,000 stars in the known universe.

410) Your hearing is less sharp after you eat too much.

411) Bread and beer were the two staples of the ancient Egyptian diet; almost everyone consumed both every day. Laborers would have a morning meal of bread, beer, and often onions, and a heartier dinner of boiled vegetables, meat, and more bread and beer.

412) The average human heart beats more than 2.5 billion times in a lifetime.

413) In humans, our two nostrils smell differently. Odors coming in through the right nostril are judged to be more pleasant, and you can describe odors coming in through your left nostril better. The difference is believed to be due to the right nostril being connected to the right brain, which deals more with emotions, and the left nostril is connected to the left brain, which deals more with language.

414) Mozart wrote numerous letters and an entire song focused on poop; no one is quite sure if it was just his odd humor or a mental issue.

415) Up through the Victorian era, it was common for both boys and girls to wear dresses until the age of seven. Boys wore dresses primarily for practical reasons; dressing and potty training were easier, and dresses weren't as easily outgrown.

416) The tallest tsunami wave ever recorded was in Lituya Bay, Alaska, in 1958; it was 1,720 feet tall. An 8.0 earthquake dropped 40 to 50 million cubic yards of rock and ice 3,000 feet down into the bay, creating the wave.

417) The furthest distance between any two points in two states is between Hawaii and Florida; it is 5,859 miles from Log Point, Elliot Key, Florida, to Kure Island, Hawaii

418) Phytophotodermatitis, also known as margarita photodermatitis, is a condition you can get from spending too much time in the sun after handling limes, lemons, or other plants containing the chemical compound furanocoumarin. In contact with exposed skin and sunlight, the compound creates a phototoxic reaction that looks and feels like a second-degree burn.

419) Flamingos bend their legs at the ankle and not the knee. Their knee is located much higher up, hidden under their feathers. The whole area from the ankle to the toes is a giant foot. The joint that looks like an ankle, near the bottom of their leg, is the beginning of their toes, so about half of what appears to be the flamingo's legs are really its feet.

420) Before the early 1500s, the color we know as orange was called geoluhread, meaning yellow-red. Orange wasn't used as a color in English until after the fruit was introduced to the British.

421) Pencils are typically yellow because it is the traditional color of Chinese royalty. In the 1890s when pencils started to be mass-produced, the best graphite came from China, and manufacturers wanted people to know they used the best quality graphite, so they painted them yellow, the color of Chinese royalty.

422) China has more bordering countries and territories than any other country; it is bordered by 14 counties and 2 territories.

423) The Appalachian Mountains used to be as tall as the Rockies and are still shrinking; meanwhile, the Himalayas used to be the size of the Rockies and are still growing.

424) Hepatitis B is the world's most common infectious disease; more than one-quarter of the world's population is infected.

425) Due to ocean circulation, the Northern Hemisphere is warmer than the Southern Hemisphere by 1.5 degrees Celsius.

426) Since the earth, our solar system, and our galaxy are all moving through space, you never have been and never will be in the same physical location twice.

427) Theodore Roosevelt had a pet hyena named Bill; he was a present from the Emperor of Ethiopia.

428) Japanese golfers have hole-in-one insurance to pay for the cost of drinks, food, and gifts they are expected to buy if they make a hole-in-one.

429) Lemons float in water; limes sink. They both have densities close to that of water, but limes are slightly denser, so they sink.

430) There are 293 possible ways to make change for a dollar.

431) In the Grimm's fairy tale, the Pied Piper of Hamelin is described as pied because he wears a two-colored coat; pied is thought to come from magpie birds, which are black and white.

432) During WWI, a Canadian soldier made a black bear his pet and named her Winnipeg. When she became a resident of the London Zoological Gardens, she was known as Winnie, and a boy named Christopher Robin, son of author A.A. Milne, adored her and named his teddy bear after her.

433) Graca Machel is the only person to be the first lady of two countries. She is the widow of both South Africa President Nelson Mandela and Mozambique President Samora Machel.

434) During the summer heat, the Eiffel Tower can grow more than six inches from metal expansion. The tower is made up of more than 7,300 tons of iron.

435) Eusocial is the highest level of sociality where animals like ants and termites have a single female or caste that produces the offspring, and nonreproductive individuals cooperate in caring for the young.

436) Sphenopalatine ganglioneuralgia is the medical term for brain freeze or ice cream headache.

437) The kakapo of New Zealand is the only flightless parrot and the heaviest parrot, weighing up to nine pounds.

438) Not including the United States, seven countries use the U.S. dollar as their official currency: Ecuador, El Salvador, Zimbabwe, Timor-Leste, Micronesia, Palau, and the Marshall Islands -.

439) The most sweat glands on the human body are on the bottom of the feet.

440) After watching workers move timber, Frank Lloyd Wright's son John invented Lincoln Logs.

441) The human brain uses about 20% of the body's oxygen and blood.

442) More English words start with the letter s than any other letter.

443) The Tour de France bicycle race has the world's most in-person spectators of any single sporting event. It attracts 12 to 15 million spectators.

444) Atoms are 99.9999999% empty space. If all the space was eliminated, the entire human species would fit into the volume of a sugar cube.

445) Canadian law requires that a skill-testing element must be included for a sweepstakes to be legal. A sweepstakes winner cannot be determined by pure luck; there must be some skill involved. The skill test is often mathematical, involving some combination of addition, subtraction, multiplication, and division that must be performed without a calculator or other aid.

446) *The Comedy of Errors* is the only Shakespeare play that mentions America.

447) Without saliva, you wouldn't be able to taste your food. Enzymes in your saliva break down the food and release molecules that are picked up by your taste buds.

448) When Colgate started mass producing its toothpaste in 1873, it was in a jar; they didn't put it in tubes until the 1890s.

449) Teeth are the only part of the human body that cannot repair itself.

450) Wooly mammoths were still alive about 900 years after the Great Pyramid of Giza was built. The last mammoths died out about 1650 BC on Wrangel Island in the Arctic Ocean; the Great Pyramid was completed in about 2560 BC.

451) When touching and microwaved, two whole grapes or a pair of beads made mostly of water concentrate the energy from the microwaves at the point where they make contact and generate a very small hot spot intense enough to spark and generate plasma. The effect seems to be dependent on the size, composition, and shape of the objects.

452) Ninety percent of all meteorites ever found come from Antarctica.

453) Four people have won two Nobel prizes: Marie Curie, Linus Pauling, John Bardeen, and Frederick Sanger.

454) New Jersey has more horses per square mile than any other state.

455) Kim is the most common surname for an Olympic athlete.

456) Frogs can't swallow with their eyes open. Since they don't have muscles to chew their food, they use their eyes to force their food down their throats. Their eyes sink inside their skull, pushing the food down.

457) Even rarer than a double rainbow, a twinned rainbow has two separate and concentric rainbow arcs splitting from a single base. Unlike a double rainbow, both rainbows have their colors in the same order. Twinned rainbows occur with a combination of different size raindrops; due to air resistance, raindrops flatten as they fall, with larger drops flattening more. If there are two rain showers with different size drops, they can combine to form a twinned rainbow.

458) In 1835, President Andrew Jackson was shot at twice at point-blank range, but he survived because both guns misfired. It was the first assassination attempt against a U.S. president.

459) The croissant originated in Austria and not France. It started in Vienna, Austria, as early as the 13th century as a denser crescent-shaped pastry called a kipferl and didn't show up in France in its current form until the early 1800s.

460) While sleeping, people burn an average of 0.42 calories an hour per pound of body weight, so a 150-pound person burns about 63 calories per hour sleeping.

461) To make it easier to give birth, hammerhead sharks are born with soft hammers bent back toward the tail.

462) Before the 20th century, lobster was considered a mark of poverty and used for fertilizer and fed to slaves. Its reputation changed when modern transportation allowed shipping live lobsters to urban centers.

463) The sound of pain around the world differs. English speakers typically say "ouch!" or "aww!"; Spanish speakers usually say "uy!" or "ay!"; French speakers say "aïe!"; Germans say "aua!" or "autsch!"; Russians say "oi!"

464) If you are locked in a completely sealed room, you will die from carbon dioxide poisoning before you die from lack of oxygen.

465) By the number of members, China has the world's largest legislature; the National People's Congress is a single house with 2,980 members.

466) Moon is the scientific name for the moon; unlike other moons in our solar system, it doesn't have any other official name.

467) Barbara Bush and Abigail Adams's husbands and sons both served as U.S. presidents.

468) In the 13th century, Pope Gregory IX believed that black cats were an instrument of Satan; he condemned cats across Europe, and they were hunted down and killed.

469) A shark can have over 30,000 teeth in its lifetime. A shark's teeth are arranged in rows, with each successive row smaller than the last. On average, they have 15 rows of teeth, with some species having up to 50 rows. The row nearest the front is the largest and most used. If a shark loses a tooth, the tooth in the row behind it moves up to take its place. A shark's teeth are not embedded in its jaw; they are attached to the skin covering the jaw. New teeth are continually being grown in a groove in the shark's mouth, and the skin moves the teeth forward into new positions. If they couldn't quickly replace their teeth, they wouldn't have been able to develop such a strong bite that causes them to lose so many teeth.

470) Of the 48 contiguous states, Olympia, Washington, is the northernmost state capital.

471) French filmmaker Albert Lamorisse (1922-1970) is best known for creating award-winning short films, such as *The Red Balloon* (1956), which won the grand prize at Cannes and an Oscar, but he also invented the strategic board game Risk in 1957.

472) As a group, musicians have the life expectancy of Zimbabwe, the lowest of any country.

473) In about 1840, naturalist Charles Darwin is credited as being the first person to put wheels on an office chair.

474) The 1815 eruption of Indonesia's Mount Tambora volcano is the most powerful explosion ever witnessed on earth. It was equivalent to 800 megatons of TNT, 14 times larger than the largest man-made explosion.

475) Philip Noel-Baker is the only Olympic medalist to also win a Nobel Prize. He won a silver medal in the 1500-meter run in 1920 and the Nobel Peace Prize in 1959.

476) The Statue of Liberty's shoe size would be 879.

477) Mozart and Beethoven composed music for the glass armonica instrument, which was invented by Benjamin Franklin. It replicated the sound a wet finger makes when rubbed along the rim of a glass; it became very popular, and several composers wrote pieces for it.

478) Polo is played on the largest field of any sport; the field is 300 yards by 160 yards.

479) In 1999 in North Carolina, a female skydiver's life was saved when her chutes didn't open and she landed on a mound of fire ants. She was jumping from 14,500 feet when her main parachute didn't open; her backup chute opened at 700 feet and quickly deflated. She hit the ground at about 80 mph, landing on a mound of fire ants that bit her over 200 times. Fire ants have a toxin-filled painful bite that can cause death in some cases. In this case, doctors determined that the repeated fire ant stings shocked her heart and stimulated her nerves, keeping her heart beating and her organs functioning long enough to reach a hospital. She suffered shattered bones and was in a coma for two weeks, but she recovered fully.

480) Only Michael Jackson, Madonna, U2, and Weird Al Yankovic have had top 40 hits in each of the last four complete decades (the 1980s, 1990s, 2000s, and 2010s).

481) When the first tea bags were developed, the idea was that customers would remove the tea from the bags, but they preferred to brew the tea in the bag.

482) St. Lucia is the only country named after a woman; it is in the Caribbean and is named after St. Lucy of Syracuse, who lived in the 3rd century.

483) King James IV of Scotland paid people so that he could practice dentistry on them. He was an amateur dentist and very interested in medicine; he established the Royal College of Surgeons in Scotland two centuries before it was established in England.

484) If they can't find food, ribbon worms will eat themselves. They can eat a substantial portion of their body and still survive.

485) Since 1980, the birthrate for human twins has increased by about 75%. Part of the reason is that older mothers are more likely to have twins.

486) Walnuts, almonds, pecans, and cashews aren't technically nuts; they are drupes, which also include peaches, plums, and cherries. Drupes are a type of fruit where an outer fleshy part surrounds a shell or pit with a seed inside. For some drupes, you eat the fleshy part, and for some, you eat the seed inside.

487) Kobe Bryant is the only person to win an Olympic gold medal and an Oscar. He won Olympic basketball gold medals in 2008 and 2012 and the Best Animated Short Film Oscar for *Dear Basketball* (2018).

488) The time between the Stegosaurus and Tyrannosaurus Rex is larger than the time between the Tyrannosaurus and you. Stegosaurus existed about 150 million years ago; Tyrannosaurus Rex didn't evolve until about 67 million years ago, so the two were separated by about 83 million years.

489) Sleeping on the job is acceptable in Japan because it is viewed as exhaustion from working hard.

490) Santa Fe, New Mexico, is the only two-word state capital in a two-word state.

491) There is a southern version of the aurora borealis (northern lights) called the aurora australis; it can be seen from Antarctica, New Zealand, Argentina, and Australia.

492) Ulage is the unfilled space between a bottle top and the liquid inside.

493) Uranus' moons are named after characters created by William Shakespeare and Alexander Pope. There are 27 moons: Cordelia, Ophelia, Bianca, Cressida, Desdemona, Juliet, Portia, Rosalind, Cupid, Belinda, Perdita, Puck, Mab, Miranda, Ariel, Umbriel, Titania, Oberon, Francisco, Caliban, Stephano, Trinculo, Sycorax, Margaret, Prospero, Setebos, and Ferdinand.

494) No witches were burned at the stake during the Salem witch trials; 20 were executed, but most were hung, and none were burned.

495) Oscar Zoroaster Phadrig Isaac Norman Henkle Emmannuel Ambroise Diggs is the real name of The Wizard of Oz.

496) Mount Rushmore cost less than $1 million to build; construction took 14 years, from 1927 to 1941, and employed 400 people.

497) Crocodiles don't sweat; they open their mouth, similar to panting, to keep cool.

498) An ambigram is a word, art form, or other symbolic representation whose elements retain meaning when viewed or interpreted from a different direction, perspective, or orientation. For example, the word "swims" is the same when it is rotated 180 degrees.

499) Through a process called REM atonia, people don't sneeze while they sleep because the brain shuts down the reflexes that would result in a sneeze.

500) Its purpose isn't known, but about 39% of the population has a bone in their knee called the fabella. From historical studies, the percentage fell from 17% in 1875 to 11% in 1918, before rising to the current number.

501) High heels were created in ancient Egypt to keep butcher's feet out of the blood. They became more popular when Persian nobility used them when riding horses to help them stay in their stirrups.

502) Many U.S. police departments adopted navy blue uniforms because they were surplus army uniforms from the Civil War.

503) The point in the ocean furthest from the nearest land is 1,670 miles from land; it is called Point Nemo and is in the South Pacific.

504) The Brooklyn Bridge was under construction when Custer was defeated at the Battle of Little Bighorn in 1876.

505) No one is born a citizen of Vatican City. To become a citizen, you must work for the city-state. If you lose your job, your citizenship is revoked, and you automatically become an Italian citizen if you aren't already a citizen of another country.

506) In about 300 BC, the Roman censor Appius Claudius Caecus removed the letter z from the alphabet because it wasn't used that much and had become archaic. It took about 200 years for it to get added back.

507) Rio de Janeiro, Brazil, was the only European capital outside of Europe; it was the capital of Portugal from 1808 to 1822. Napoleon was invading Portugal at the time, so the Portuguese royal family moved to Rio de Janeiro, and it became the capital.

508) The last guillotining in France occurred on September 10, 1977.

509) In the second half of the 18th century to study the health effects of coffee, King Gustav III of Sweden commuted the death sentence of a pair of twins, on the condition that one drank three pots of coffee each day for the rest of their life and one drank three pots of tea each day. He appointed two doctors to supervise the experiment; both doctors and the king died before the experiment was complete. The tea-drinking twin died first, at age 83.

510) Leonardo da Vinci could write with both his left and right hand simultaneously.

511) The longest recorded time a chicken has flown continuously is 13 seconds; the longest distance chicken flight ever recorded is 301.5 feet.

512) Only three people have won individual gold medals in the same event in four consecutive Olympics: Michael Phelps (swimming 200-meter individual medley), Carl Lewis (long jump), and Al Oerter (discus).

513) Mushrooms are more closely related to humans than they are to plants. Animals and fungi branched off from plants about 1.1 billion years ago; later, animals and fungi separated genealogically, making mushrooms closer to humans than to plants.

514) The pineal gland is the smallest organ in the human body; it is about the size of a grain of rice and is located in the center of the brain.

515) A vast reservoir of water, three times the volume of all the oceans, is located about 400 miles beneath the earth's crust. The water is locked up in a mineral called ringwoodite.

516) On average, domestic cats sleep 15 hours per day.

517) In 1898, Morgan Robertson wrote a short novel called *Futility*. It had the *Titan*, a large unsinkable ship that carried an insufficient number of lifeboats, and on an April voyage, it hits an iceberg and sinks in the North Atlantic, resulting in the loss of most everyone on board. Fourteen years later in April 1912, the large unsinkable *Titanic*, with an insufficient number of lifeboats, hit an iceberg and sank in the North Atlantic, losing most of the people on board.

518) There were 20 years between the first female in space and the first American female in space. Soviet Valentina Tereshkova was the first in 1963; Sally Ride was the first American in 1983.

519) Russia is the third closest country to the United States.

520) It is illegal for drug companies to advertise directly to consumers almost everywhere in the world, except in the United States and New Zealand.

521) The sign we know as the ampersand (&) was the 27th letter of the English alphabet before being dropped. It wasn't called an ampersand at that time and was referred to as "and."

522) The ZIP in ZIP Code stands for Zone Improvement Plan.

523) Dunce caps originally were a sign of intelligence. Thirteenth-century philosopher John Duns Scotus created the idea of the pointy hat as a reverse funnel to spread knowledge into the brain; the hats became popular and a symbol of high intelligence. In the 1500s, Scotus' ideas fell out of favor, and the pointy hat eventually came to mean the opposite.

524) The ancient Romans threw walnuts at weddings; they signified hopes for the fertility of the bride.

525) The letter x begins the fewest words in the English language.

526) By 70 years of age, the average person will have shed 105 pounds of skin.

527) Birds don't urinate. They convert excess nitrogen to uric acid, instead of urea; it is less toxic and doesn't need to be diluted as much. It goes out with their other waste and saves water, so they don't have to drink as much.

528) The Pentagon, headquarters for the U.S. Department of Defense, was originally designed to fit on a piece of land that was bordered on five sides by roads. The original site was too close to Arlington Cemetery, so it was moved to its current location. Since the design was already complete, it was slightly modified, but it kept its pentagon shape, even though it wasn't essential any longer.

529) Coprophagy is the act of eating your own poop. Rats and most rodents have simple digestive systems and eat their own poop to recover additional nutrients.

530) Windsor Castle is 590,000 square feet, making it the world's largest inhabited castle.

531) Libya is 99% desert, the highest percentage of any country.

532) In 1943, the Slinky was invented accidentally by Richard James, a mechanical engineer. He was devising springs that could keep sensitive ship equipment steady at sea, and after accidentally knocking some samples off a shelf, he saw a spring right itself.

533) Your fingers don't contain any muscles. The muscles that bend the finger joints are in the palm and mid-forearm and are connected to the finger bones by tendons that pull on and move the fingers.

534) Based on the volume of the average human body, the world's population could fit in a cube of 2,577 feet on each side, about 0.116 cubic miles.

535) Ostrakismos, meaning ostracism, was a process in ancient Greece where any citizen could be voted out and expelled for 10 years. In some instances, it was used to express popular anger against an individual, but it was often used preemptively to remove someone who was thought to be a threat to the state.

536) *Rocky*, *Chariots of Fire*, and *Million Dollar Baby* are the only three sports-related movies that have won the Best Picture Oscar.

537) At 4,300 miles long, the Andes are the world's longest above-water mountain range, but the mid-ocean ridge, at 25,097 miles, is the longest if you include underwater ranges. The mid-ocean ridges of all the world's oceans are connected.

538) Hong Kong has more skyscrapers than any other city; New York City is second; Dubai is third. There is no exact definition of a skyscraper, but they are generally considered to be 150 meters or taller.

539) There is a very rare third type of human twin called sesquizygous (semi-identical). Monozygotic (identical) twins result from a single fertilized egg that splits in two and forms two identical boys or two identical girls that share 100% of their DNA. Dizygotic (fraternal) twins form from two eggs that have been fertilized by two of the father's sperm, creating two genetically unique siblings that share 50% of their DNA. Semi-identical twins are so rare that only two cases have ever been identified; they share between 50% and 100% of their DNA and are formed when a single egg is fertilized by two sperm. This shouldn't happen; once a sperm enters the egg, the egg locks down to prevent another sperm from entering. Even if a second sperm entered, an embryo with three, rather than the normal two, sets of chromosomes won't survive. To produce semi-identical twins, the egg splits the three sets of chromosomes into two separate cell sets.

540) English has more words than any other language.

541) Fruit flies were the very first animal to go into space. In 1947, they went up in a captured German V2 rocket; they were recovered alive.

542) Montpelier, Vermont, is the only state capital without a McDonald's.

543) NASA accidentally erased and reused the original 1969 *Apollo 11* moon landing tapes. The tapes were reused as part of a money-saving effort.

544) Genghis Khan fathered countless children; while we will never know exactly how many offspring the Mongol leader had; scientists now believe that about 1 in every 200 men are his direct descendants.

545) Due to its unique chemical qualities, honey can remain edible for centuries; 3,000-year-old edible honey has been found in tombs.

546) Academy Awards are called Oscars because Margaret Herrick, Academy librarian and future executive director, thought the statue looked like her uncle Oscar.

547) The first pedestrian ever killed by a car occurred on August 17, 1896. Bridget Driscoll was struck by a demonstration car that was traveling at 4 mph.

548) The longest gloved boxing match in history was in 1893 and lasted for 110 three-minute rounds, for a total of 7 hours and 19 minutes. It was a lightweight match between Andy Bowen and Jack Burke in New Orleans, Louisiana, and began around 9 p.m. and finished after 4 a.m. There was no winner, as both fighters were too exhausted to continue.

549) Approximately 88% of the world's population lives in the Northern Hemisphere. About half of the world's population lives north of 27 degrees north latitude.

550) Based on the number of participants, soccer is the world's most popular sport; badminton is second, and field hockey is third.

551) William Howard Taft is the only man to have been both Chief Justice of the U.S. Supreme Court and U.S. president.

552) Unconsciously, native English speakers say adjectives preceding nouns in a specific order: opinion, size, age, shape, color, origin, material, and purpose. That is why we say things instinctively like "big, old, black, leather chair" instead of "black, leather, old, big chair," which doesn't sound right.

553) At some points in history, money was designed to discourage people from having too much. According to Greek historian Plutarch, the Spartans used long, heavy iron rods as their currency to discourage people from pursuing great wealth. The currency was called obeloi and was so cumbersome that carrying multiple pieces required help.

554) Written out in English, eight billion is the second number alphabetically, no matter how high you go.

555) An average alligator can go through 2,000 to 3,000 teeth in a lifetime. An alligator has roughly 80 teeth, and as the teeth wear down, they are replaced.

556) Piggy banks got their name because they were originally made from pygg, an orange-colored clay. During the Middle Ages, the clay was used to make bowls, jars, and other containers that people started to store change in; the containers were not made into pig shapes until much later.

557) The standard U.S. railroad width of 4 feet 8.5 inches is directly derived from the width of Roman war chariots. The English expatriates who designed the U.S. railroad system based their measurements on the pre-railroad tramways built in England, which were built using the same tools used to build wagons. To avoid breaking down during long treks across the old English roads created by the Romans, wagons were built to fit the ruts carved out by Roman war chariots, and all Roman chariots were built to a standard width of 4 feet 8.5 inches.

558) The pizza served in the United States each day would cover an area of about 100 acres.

559) Chocolate is the only edible substance that melts just below human body temperature. Chocolate melts at 93 degrees, which is why it melts in your mouth.

560) Cassowaries are the world's second-largest bird, standing up to 6 feet tall and weighing up to 130 pounds. They are also one of the most dangerous birds, with a four-inch, dagger-like claw on each foot that can slice open a predator with a single kick, and they have killed humans. They can run up to 31 mph and are native to the tropical forests of Papua New Guinea, Indonesia, and northeastern Australia.

561) At one point in the year, it is the same local time for people living in Oregon and Florida. A small part of eastern Oregon is in the Mountain Time Zone, and a small part of western Florida is in the Central Time Zone. When the change from daylight saving time to standard time is made, these two areas share the same time for one hour after the Central Time Zone has fallen back to standard time and before the Mountain Time Zone has.

562) Albert Einstein's 1921 Nobel Prize in Physics was for the photoelectric effect, not for his work on relativity. He suggested for the first time that light is both a wave and a particle and established the existence of photons.

563) Greenland is part of the Kingdom of Denmark; if you include it as part of Denmark's area, Denmark is the 12th largest country.

564) Ecuador is the only point on the equator with snow on the ground.

565) In 1941, the first U.S. television commercial ever broadcast was for Bulova watches.

566) Cicadas flex their muscles to buckle a series of ribs, one after another, to produce their loud sound. Every time a rib buckles, it produces a click; many clicks produce the buzzing sound. The series of ribs are called a tymbal.

567) Hippo milk is bright pink. Hippos secrete two unique acids, hipposudoric acid and norhipposudoric acid, that function as a natural sunscreen and antimicrobial agent. The acids are red and orange, and when mixed with a hippo mother's milk, they turn it bright pink.

568) The Statue of Liberty is made of copper; about 62,000 pounds of copper were used to create it, and it looked like a new penny when it was first created.

569) A pangram is a sentence or verse that contains all letters in the alphabet at least once, such as "The quick brown fox jumps over a lazy dog."

570) The use of the word "bucks" for dollars dates to the 1700s when deerskins were commonly used for trading. A trading record from 1748 notes the exchange of a cask of whiskey for 5 bucks. The term stayed around after the dollar became the U.S. standard currency in 1792.

571) The difference between antlers (found on deer, elk, and moose) and horns (found on pronghorn antelope, bighorn sheep, and bison) is that antlers are an extension of the animal's skull, and they are true bone that is shed and regrown each year. Horns are composed of an interior bone that is an extension of the skull; they are covered by an exterior sheath, grown by specialized hair follicles. They aren't shed and continue to grow throughout the animal's life. The exception is the pronghorn antelope that sheds and regrows its horn sheath each year.

572) Sharks have been around longer than trees. The first sharks appeared about 450 million years ago; the first trees were about 385 million years ago.

573) A male dog lifts his leg to pee because he wants to leave his mark as high as possible, as a sign of size and status. He also prefers to pee on vertical objects because the scent lasts longer.

574) Researchers have found that cats can recognize their names, but they are also willing to ignore you.

575) Human babies are born without kneecaps; at three to five years old, the cartilage in their knee ossifies into kneecaps.

576) Snails move at a steady pace with a maximum speed of about 50 yards per hour, or 0.03 mph.

577) The whip was the first man-made object to break the sound barrier. The crack a whip makes is due to a small sonic boom.

578) A blue moon is defined as the second full moon in a calendar month. It happens about every three years, giving the expression "once in a blue moon" for something that doesn't occur very often.

579) Even though William Shakespeare has become the accepted spelling of the writer's name, he never once spelled it that way, and it was spelled in over 80 variations by his contemporaries, including several by Shakespeare himself.

580) Even though it is known worldwide for its casinos, Monaco doesn't allow its citizens to even step foot in its casinos unless they work there. This law excludes foreign nationals that reside in Monaco and account for about 80% of the population.

581) A double rainbow happens when light is reflected twice in the raindrop. You see two different reflections coming from different angles, and it also reverses the order of the colors on the secondary rainbow.

582) In the 15th century, King Louis XI of France ordered Abbot de Beigne to create a musical instrument using the voices of pigs. He built a keyboard that jabbed a spike into the rumps of pigs to produce a squeal.

583) In 1964, grad student Donal Rusk Currey got his tree corer stuck in a bristlecone pine, and a park ranger helped him remove the tool by cutting the tree down. When Currey counted the rings, he found out the tree was almost 5,000 years old, the oldest ever recorded at that time.

584) Male giraffes determine whether a female is fertile and ready to mate by tasting her urine. The male bumps the female until she urinates and then tastes the urine for hormones, indicating she is in heat.

585) The Meganeura is the largest known flying insect ever. It lived more than 300 million years ago during the Carboniferous Period and was a dragonfly-like insect with a wingspan of about 2.5 feet. It was a carnivore and fed on other insects and small amphibians.

586) To ensure global supply in the case of an emergency, Canada has a strategic maple syrup reserve. The reserve contains about 2.4 million gallons of syrup. Quebec province produces about 75% of the global supply of maple syrup.

587) Deaf-mute player William Hoy inspired the non-verbal signs used in baseball and stole over 600 bases in his career; he started his career in 1888.

588) Until the 19th century, the word hypocrites referred to actors.

589) Human bodies can continue to move for more than a year after death. Through time-lapse photography, researchers found that bodies can continue to move significantly; the movements are believed to be due to the process of decomposition as the body mummifies and the ligaments dry out.

590) Of cities of 1 million or more population, Auckland, New Zealand, is furthest away from another city of 1 million or more population; it is 1,347 miles away from Sydney, Australia.

591) English is the official language of the most countries.

592) In traditional vampire folklore, one of their weaknesses is arithmomania, a compulsion to count things. This weakness can be used to defend against them by placing grains of rice or sand out that they will be compelled to count. Therefore, *Sesame Street's* Count von Count's love of counting is part of being a vampire.

593) Beetles are the most common group of insects. Flies are the second most common, and bees and ants are third.

594) The first automobile speeding ticket was issued in 1896 in England. The car was going 8 mph; the speed limit for cars was 2 mph. You could go over 2 mph if you had someone walk in front of the car waving a red flag to alert people.

595) In the 14th century, the bubonic plague killed so many people that the world population did not reach the same levels again until the 17th century.

596) Starfish don't have blood; their circulatory system is primarily made of seawater.

597) Sea otters hold hands while they are sleeping, so they don't drift apart.

598) The Tower of Pisa took 177 years to build, but it started leaning, due to soil subsidence, just 10 years after its completion in 1372. The lean was 5.5 degrees before a 2010 restoration reduced it to 4 degrees.

599) The tongue is the fastest healing part of the human body.

600) Mars is red because it is covered in iron oxide (rust).

601) Pizza Hut is the oldest pizza chain in the United States; it was founded in 1958.

602) The tall, pleated chef's hat is called a toque; the 100 folds in the toque are said to represent 100 ways to cook an egg.

603) American Eddie Eagan is the only person to win gold medals in both the Winter and Summer Olympics. He won for boxing in 1920 and bobsled in 1932.

604) Built between 1825 and 1843, the world's first underwater tunnel was under London's Thames River.

605) If you wrote out every number in English (one, two, three, etc.), you wouldn't use the letter b until you reached one billion.

606) The average person walks about 75,000 miles in their life.

607) Mark Twain was the first novelist to present a typed manuscript to their publisher.

608) The Declaration of Independence wasn't signed on July 4, 1776. It was signed on August 2, 1776; it was adopted by Congress on July 4, 1776.

609) On a per-capita basis, Alaska produces more serial killers than any other state.

610) Early Americans used corn cobs for toilet paper. Dried corncobs were plentiful, efficient, and softer and more flexible than you might think.

611) An autological word is a word that describes itself; some examples include word, noun, polysyllabic, unhyphenated, and suffixed.

612) The word deadline originated in American Civil War prison camps; it was the line that prisoners couldn't go beyond, or they would be shot.

613) The Arabian Desert contains the world's largest continuous body of sand. The contiguous sand body, known as the Rub 'al-Khali or the "Empty Quarter," is about 250,966 square miles.

614) South Africa has three national capital cities. Pretoria is the administrative capital; Cape Town is the legislative capital, and Bloemfontein is the judicial capital.

615) Pareidolia is the term for seeing patterns in random data. Some common examples are seeing a likeness in the clouds or an image on the surface of the moon.

616) Nudiustertian means the day before yesterday.

617) The Sargasso Sea is the only sea without a coastline (no land border). It is in the North Atlantic, off the coast of the United States, and is defined by currents.

618) TV dinners were first sold in 1954. Swanson had 260 tons of leftover frozen turkeys from Thanksgiving. Inspired by the food trays on airlines, they created a meal of turkey, cornbread dressing, gravy, peas, and sweet potatoes.

619) More national capital cities start with the letter "B" than any other letter: Baghdad, Baku, Bamako, Bandar Seri Begawan, Bangkok, Bangui, Banjul, Basseterre, Beijing, Beirut, Belgrade, Belmopan, Berlin, Bern, Bishkek, Bissau, Bogotá, Brasília, Bratislava, Brazzaville, Bridgetown, Brussels, Bucharest, Budapest, and Buenos Aires.

620) Osmium is the densest naturally occurring element; it is about 25 times denser than water.

621) As part of its reproductive process, the jewel wasp will sting a cockroach twice, first in the thorax to partially immobilize it and then in the head to block its normal escape reflex. The wasp is too small to carry the cockroach, so it leads it back to its burrow by pulling on one of its antennae. Once in the burrow, the wasp lays one egg on the roach's abdomen and exits and fills in the burrow entrance with pebbles. With the effect of the wasp venom, the roach rests in the burrow, and in about three days, the wasp's egg hatches, and the larva begins feeding on the roach for four to five days before chewing its way into the roach's abdomen. It continues to reside inside the roach, and over eight days, it consumes the roach's internal organs in an order that maximizes the time the roach is still alive. The larva enters a pupal stage and forms a cocoon inside the roach, and the fully-grown wasp eventually emerges from the roach's body, completing the reproductive cycle.

622) Portland cement gets its name from England. It was created in the mid-19th century and is named because of its similarity to Portland stone that was quarried on the Isle of Portland, off the coast of England.

623) Phoenix, Arizona, has the largest population of any state capital.

624) Benjamin Franklin was carried to the U.S. Constitutional Convention in a sedan chair carried by prisoners.

625) Sunsets on Mars are blue.

626) Jupiter is the fastest spinning planet in our solar system; at the equator, it rotates at 28,273 mph; comparatively, the Earth rotates at 1,038 mph.

627) In Iceland, you can swim between the European and North American tectonic plates. The Silfra fissure is a crack between the two continental plates and is the only spot in the world where you can swim directly between the North American and European continents. The crack is filled with extremely clear, cold water that remains about 35 to 39 degrees Fahrenheit all year.

628) Thomas Jefferson wrote his own translation of the Bible. He didn't agree with some of the supernatural elements of the Bible and wrote his own version, eliminating what he didn't agree with.

629) Blind people still dream. People who were born blind or lost their sight at four to five years old or younger don't have visual imagery in their dreams, but people who lost their sight later in life continue to dream with visual imagery as if they could still see.

630) Worldwide, the average human weighs about 137 pounds.

631) The Red-billed Quelea, a sparrow-sized bird found in sub-Saharan Africa, is the world's most abundant wild bird species. Their population is estimated at 1.5 billion.

632) The sport of cricket originated the term hat trick. The term first appeared in 1858 when H. H. Stephenson took three wickets with three consecutive balls; fans held a collection for him and presented him with a hat, which was bought with the proceeds.

633) As a gas, oxygen is odorless and colorless; in its liquid and solid forms, it looks pale blue.

634) Paraguay is the only country with a two-sided (different designs on each side) flag.

635) A desert locust swarm can cover 460 square miles and contain billions of locusts that can eat their weight in plants each day, consuming potentially hundreds of millions of pounds of vegetation per day.

636) Extant is the opposite of extinct.

637) The ostrich is the only animal with two kneecaps on each knee.

638) Charles Darwin ate many of the animal species he discovered.

639) Boston and Austin are the only two U.S. state capitals with rhyming names.

640) At a cost of $160 billion, the International Space Station is the most expensive man-made object ever built.

641) Men wore high heels before women did; it was a sign of status. In the 1600s, women started to wear high heels as a way of appropriating masculine power; it then filtered down to the lower classes. When it was no longer a power symbol, men eventually quit wearing high heels.

642) When you wake up with a jolt, it is called a hypnic jerk. It is an involuntary twitch that occurs when you are beginning to fall asleep, causing you to jump and awaken suddenly for a moment.

643) There are 45 miles of nerves in the human body.

644) The mouthwash Listerine was created as a surgical disinfectant.

645) The Brothers Grimm version of *Cinderella* is a much darker story. To fit into the shoe, the stepsisters cut off their toe and a part of their heel, and they try to go to Cinderella's wedding and get their eyes plucked out by birds.

646) Bug spray doesn't repel mosquitos. Ingredients like DEET mask what you smell like, creating a barrier on your skin that interferes with the mosquito's detection of the lactic acid and carbon dioxide they're attracted to.

647) One million dollars in $100 bills weighs about 20.4 pounds.

648) The can opener was invented 45 years after tin cans were invented.

649) The Russian army didn't wear socks until 2013. Since the 17th century, the army had worn portyanki, a square of cloth (cotton for summer, flannel for winter), that they wrapped their feet in. Portyanki were far cheaper to make than socks, and they were quicker and easier to wash, dry, and mend, but they did have to be worn correctly and wrapped tightly, or they could cause blisters. You also had to be able to put your portyanki on fast; regulations required soldiers to be fully dressed in 45 seconds.

650) In 1892, Gallaudet University, a school for the deaf, originated the football huddle. They huddled to avoid the other team seeing their sign language.

651) Ice worms are related to common earthworms, but they spend their entire lives in glaciers and require below-freezing temperatures to survive. They are found across the northern United States and Canada and come to the glacier surface to feed on snow algae. At temperatures even five degrees above freezing, their internal membranes start to fall apart, and they essentially liquefy and die.

652) Macy's was the first U.S. department store; it opened in 1858.

653) In Switzerland, it is illegal to own just one guinea pig. They are social animals, and it is considered animal cruelty to deny them companionship.

654) The oldest known advertising dates from about 3,000 BC. In Thebes, Greece, a fabric seller announced a reward for the return of his slave to his store, where the most beautiful fabrics are woven for each person's taste.

655) The Amazon River has the world's largest discharge volume. At an average of about 55 million gallons per second, its discharge is larger than the world's next seven largest rivers combined and accounts for 20% of the total global river discharge to the oceans.

656) Time, person, and year are the three most used English nouns.

657) Up until a 1747 proclamation by Spain's King Ferdinand VI, many Europeans believed California was an island. The misconception started in 1510 when Spanish novelist Garci Rodríguez de Montalvo wrote *Las Sergas de Esplandián*, a novel about a mythical island called California. His work formed the basis for naming California, and the name propagated the idea it was an island.

658) Antepenultimate means the third to last thing.

659) Boxing originated the term southpaw. Left-handed fighters were said to use a southpaw stance; no one is quite sure why. Hitting someone with a left came to be known as a southpaw punch.

660) At the Palace of Versailles, there were no restrooms, so people would just defecate in the corners. Visitors often complained about how bad the palace smelled, and King Louis XIV ordered that the hallways be cleaned of feces at least once a week, and they brought in potted orange trees to mask the smell.

661) The probability that any single glass of water contains at least one molecule of water drunk by Cleopatra is almost 100%. There are about 1,000 times as many molecules of water in a glass as there are glasses of water in the earth's water supply. If water molecules spread through the entire water supply, any given glass of water should contain 1,000 molecules of water from any other glass.

662) Moths rest with their wings open flat; butterflies rest with their wings together.

663) The lunula is the white crescent near the base of your fingernail.

664) Some spiders produce a milk-like substance for their young. Researchers have found that the jumping spider secretes a nutritious milk-like substance to feed its offspring. The spider also continues to care for its young as they mature and become independent, so maternal care may be more widespread than has been assumed in the animal world.

665) Until they are about four months old, human babies only see in black and white with shades of gray.

666) Andrew Jackson is the only U.S. president who was held as a prisoner of war; he joined the Revolutionary War at age 13 and was captured by the British.

667) A sneeze sounds different in different parts of the world. Americans typically say "achoo!"; for Germans, it is "hatschi!"; for Spanish, it is "achis!"; for Japanese, it is "hakashun!"; for Russians, it is "apchkhi!"; for French, it is "atchoum!"

668) The largest cell in the human body is the egg; it is about 30 times larger than the smallest cell, the sperm.

669) Other than leap day, the least common U.S. birthday is December 25.

670) The king cobra is the only snake that builds a nest. They can lay up to 40 eggs at once; the nest is built from vegetation and helps keep the eggs safe.

671) In terms of how long it takes to process input, the fastest human sense is hearing; it takes as little as 0.05 seconds to process.

672) The tardigrade is a water-dwelling, eight-legged, micro animal about 0.02 inches long that can survive extreme conditions that would kill most life forms. They can survive temperatures from -458 to 300 degrees Fahrenheit, pressures from the vacuum of space to more than 1,000 atmospheres, and radiation 1,000 times higher than other animals. They can also live for 30 years without food or water. They were discovered in 1773 and are found everywhere from mountain tops to deep sea and tropical areas to the Antarctic.

673) On average, the moon is 238,900 miles from the earth.

674) The disclaimer that appears at the end of virtually every film that states the movie is a work of fiction and any similarity to actual persons living or dead or actual events is purely coincidental is due to Rasputin's murder. In the 1933 MGM film *Rasputin and the Empress*, Felix Yusupov, the man who assassinated Rasputin, and his wife Irina were portrayed under different names, and they were both still alive. They were unhappy with how they were portrayed, but since Felix had confessed to the killing, it was more difficult to prove a libel case around him, so Irina sued the studio for libel and won. Part of the problem for MGM was that they implied at the

beginning of the film that it depicted real people and events. A judge in the case told MGM that the studio would have stood a better chance had they incorporated a disclaimer stating the opposite, so that is why the disclaimer exists on films today.

675) In 1912, Merck invented the drug ecstasy. They wanted to develop something to stop abnormal bleeding, and they synthesized MDMA to avoid a Bayer patent. There was no real interest in the drug at the time, and it wasn't until 1975 that the psychoactive effects of the drug were seriously considered.

676) Your taste buds are replaced every 10-14 days.

677) The name M&M's stands for Mars & Murrie, the co-creators of the candy. Forest Mars, son of the Mars Company founder, and Bruce Murrie, son of the Hershey Chocolate president, went into business together in 1941 to develop the candy. Until 1949 when the partners had a falling out and Mars bought back Murrie's share of the business, M&M's contained Hershey's chocolate.

678) The Greenland shark has the longest known lifespan of all vertebrate (with a backbone) animal species. They can live up to 400 years.

679) A female cat is called a molly; after she becomes a mother, she is called a queen.

680) Apple founder Steve Jobs was adopted at birth; later in life, he decided to find his biological family. He found his mother and sister, and his sister found their father, a Syrian immigrant and California restaurant owner. When his sister went to meet their father, Jobs asked her not to mention anything about him. When talking to her father, he mentioned that famous people came to his restaurant and mentioned Steve Jobs as one of them. When his sister told Jobs of this, he remembered meeting the restaurant owner multiple times. The two never met in person after knowing who each other was.

681) A group of rattlesnakes is called a rhumba.

682) According to recent studies, there may be about one trillion species of microbes, and 99.999% of them have yet to be discovered.

683) The sun has made about 20 orbits around the center of the Milky Way Galaxy in its life.

684) Mercury was used in the production of felt used in hats; this led to the expression "mad as a hatter," due to mercury poisoning.

685) The Amazon is the world's widest river; it is almost 25 miles wide during the wet season.

686) In 1838, Edgar Allan Poe published the novel *The Narrative of Arthur Gordon Pym of Nantucket* that describes how the crew of a ship called the *Grampus* were adrift in the ocean and drew straws to decide who would be eaten. The losing crew member was Richard Parker, who was killed and eaten. Forty-six years later in 1884, a yacht called the *Mignonette* sank, and its four surviving crew escaped in a lifeboat. They eventually decided they were going to have to eat one of their own to survive. They killed and ate a crew member named Richard Parker.

687) In 1866 in the last battle Liechtenstein ever participated in, they sent out an army of 80 men for the Austro-Prussian War; they came back with 81 men. They had no casualties and picked up an extra soldier along the way.

688) Fortune cookies were invented in the United States.

689) The tarsier has the largest eye relative to its body of any mammal. It is a small primate found on various Southeast Asian islands, including the Philippines. It is known for its extremely large eyes; even though it is about the size of a squirrel, each eye has a diameter of about 0.6 inches, as large as its brain.

690) The monkeys Mizaru, Kikazaru, and Iwazaru are better known as see no evil, hear no evil, and speak no evil.

691) With speeds up to 68 mph, the sailfish is the fastest fish.

692) Amen is in 1,200 different languages without change.

693) Mosquitos don't have teeth, but a mosquito's proboscis has 47 sharp edges on its tip that help it cut through skin and even clothing. The pain you feel from a mosquito bite is from the initial stab of sticking its proboscis into you.

694) In August 1864, Abraham Lincoln was riding a horse to the Soldiers' Home outside of Washington, D.C., where the president and his family stayed to escape the summer heat. There was a gunshot, and his horse bolted; Lincoln lost his hat, which he believed was due to his horse jerking. When they went back to find his hat, they found a bullet hole in it; the assassination attempt was about eight months before John Wilkes Booth assassinated Lincoln.

695) Without even flapping their wings, the wandering albatross can travel 500-600 miles in a single day and maintain speeds higher than 79 mph for more than 8 hours. They do it through a cycle called dynamic soaring that has four major components: a windward climb, a turn from windward to leeward at the flight's peak, a leeward descent, and a curve from leeward to windward at the flight's base.

696) *Sesame Street's* Big Bird is 8'2" tall.

697) Ohio's Kenyon College won the NCAA Division III men's swimming and diving championship for 31 consecutive years (1980-2010). It is the most consecutive national championships for any men's or women's team in any NCAA division.

698) In 1828, Ioannis Kapodistriasthe, the first governor of Greece, spread the potato as a Greek crop by getting people to steal them. He tried to introduce potatoes as a crop to help with the Greek hunger problem, but when he offered potatoes to anyone interested, no one wanted them, so he ordered the shipment of potatoes put on public display under guard. People assumed the potatoes must be important since they were guarded and began to steal them, which the guards allowed. They took all the potatoes and spread the potato as a Greek crop.

699) From the mid-5th to the early 13th century, Constantinople was one of the largest and wealthiest cities in Europe. It had survived many attacks and sieges and was regarded as one of the most impregnable cities, with an outer ditch and three rings of walls. In 1453, the city was besieged by the Turks, and someone accidentally left one of the small gates open, allowing the Turks to get in. The city may have fallen regardless, but the open gate quickened its demise. The inhabitants were killed or enslaved, and Emperor Constantine XI was killed.

700) We don't know how many insect species exist; new beetles are discovered at a rate of one an hour. There are 350,000 named beetles, plus perhaps 8 million more unnamed.

701) The placebo effect works even if people know it is a placebo. In studies, if people were told the pill they were taking was a placebo but were also told that placebos can have an effect, they experienced the same outcome as those unknowingly taking a placebo.

702) In 1861, Abraham Lincoln imposed the first U.S. federal income tax. It was implemented to pay for the Civil War.

703) Alaska has about 365,000 miles of rivers, more than any other state and almost twice as much as second-place Texas.

704) Humans have managed to explore only about 5% of the ocean floor.

705) It is illegal to take pictures of the Eiffel Tower at night. French copyright law gives the original creator of an object exclusive rights to its sale and distribution; this includes buildings and lasts for 70 years after death. Gustave Eiffel, the tower creator, died in 1923, which means the copyright ran out in 1993. The Las Vegas replica wasn't built until 1999. However, night photos are still protected by copyright since the Eiffel Tower lights were installed in 1985 and are considered a separate artistic work by their creator, Pierre Bideau. They are protected by copyright until 70 years after his death.

706) Early versions of the computer mouse were referred to as a turtle, presumably because of its hard shell on top.

707) A rat can fall 50 feet uninjured.

708) The button on the top of a baseball cap is called a squatchee.

709) Alice in Wonderland Syndrome is a neuropsychological condition where people may perceive objects to be larger or smaller than they are or nearer or farther away than they are. It can also affect the perception of the passage of time and other senses. It is often associated with migraines, brain tumors, and psychoactive drug use.

710) Oxford University existed about 350 years before the start of the Inca and Aztec empires. As early as 1096, there was teaching at Oxford, making it the world's third-oldest university in continuous operation and the oldest English-speaking university. The Aztec and Incan empires weren't founded until the 1430s.

711) Ancient Rome's population density was about eight times greater than modern New York City.

712) An adult blue whale's stomach can hold 2,200 pounds of krill at a time, and they require almost 9,000 pounds of krill a day.

713) When attacked, the horned toad squirts blood from its eyes.

714) With 17 million units sold, the Commodore 64, introduced in 1982 with a 1 MHz processor and 64K of memory, is the largest selling personal computer model of all time.

715) The philtrum is the groove in your upper lip that runs from the top of the lip to the nose.

716) Almost the entire continent of South America is east of the easternmost point of Florida. Mainland South America and Florida only overlap for a little more than one degree of longitude.

717) The saltwater crocodile is the world's largest reptile. They are up to 20 feet long and weigh up to 3,000 pounds.

718) According to the CDC, 50% of American adults will develop at least one mental illness in their lifetime.

719) Before 1824, no one knew that dinosaurs had existed. Although the name dinosaur wasn't applied until 1842, William Buckland, a geology professor at Oxford, was the first person to recognize dinosaurs when he used the name Megalosaurus to describe an extinct carnivorous lizard fossil.

720) In January 1919, a 50-foot-tall holding tank burst open sending a 15-foot-tall wave of molasses through the streets of Boston, Massachusetts. It crushed houses and killed 21 people and injured 150.

721) To get a narcotic hit and ward off insects, lemurs in Madagascar capture large red millipedes. When millipedes are picked up, they secrete a toxic combination of chemicals, including cyanide, as a defense mechanism. Lemurs pick up a millipede and bite it gently and throw it back on the ground. They rub the millipede secretion all over their fur, which functions as a natural pesticide and wards off malaria-carrying mosquitos. The secretion also acts as a narcotic that causes the lemurs to salivate profusely and enter a state of intoxication.

722) Ancient gladiators were mainly vegetarian; their diet was grain-based and mostly meat-free.

723) *Dune*, the bestselling science fiction book of all time, was rejected by more than 20 publishers before being published by Chilton Books, a little-known printing house best known for its auto repair manuals.

724) In the sport of curling, pebbling the rink ice is done to create friction for the stone to curl. Ice preparers sprinkle the ice with tiny water droplets that freeze on the surface of the ice, creating a pebbled texture.

725) Termites are the only insect that has both a king and a queen. The king helps found the colony with the queen and will mate with the queen during his life. There may be more than one pair of kings and queens in a termite mound.

726) $1.19 (three quarters, four dimes, and four pennies) is the most money you can have in change and not be able to make change for a dollar.

727) Arabian horses have a greater bone density than other horses; they also have a shorter back with one fewer lumbar vertebra and one fewer pair of ribs.

728) The Snickers candy bar is named after the creator's horse.

729) The world's largest gold depository is the Manhattan Federal Reserve Bank; it houses 7,700 tons of gold.

730) In 1872, P.B.S. Pinchback became the first African American state governor. He had been a Louisiana state senator and was serving as lieutenant governor when Governor Henry Clay Warmoth had to step down temporarily while he battled impeachment charges for election tampering.

Pinchback served as governor for 36 days; there wouldn't be another African American governor until 1990.

731) Astronomers have discovered the largest reservoir of water ever detected in the universe; it has the equivalent of 140 trillion times the water in the earth's oceans and surrounds a huge black hole, more than 12 billion light-years away.

732) We won't always have the same North Star. In 13,000 years, Polaris, the current North Star, will be replaced by Vega, and 26,000 years from now, Polaris will be back as the North Star. This is because the direction the earth's axis points changes due to a motion called precession. If you think of a spinning top given a slight nudge, the top traces out a cone pattern; that is how the earth moves on its axis. The earth bulges out at the equator, and the gravitational attraction of the moon and the sun on the bulge causes the precession that repeats in a 26,000-year cycle.

733) Five surnames have been shared by more than one president: Adams, Harrison, Johnson, Roosevelt, and Bush. Only Andrew and Lyndon Johnson weren't related.

734) By area, 38% of the United States is further north than the southernmost point of Canada. Middle Island, in Lake Erie at 41.7 degrees north latitude, is the southernmost point of Canada and is about the same latitude as Chicago.

735) The Ruppell's Griffon vulture is the highest-flying bird species ever recorded. They have been spotted at 37,000 feet and have special hemoglobin that makes their oxygen intake more effective.

736) As a mosquito sucks your blood, they also pee on you. As they suck blood, mosquitoes need to get rid of excess fluid and salts, so they urinate to maintain their fluid and salt balance.

737) About 100 cats roam free at Disneyland; they keep the rodent population down and have been in the park since it opened in 1955. They have feeding stations, veterinary care, and are taken care of by the workers.

738) A digamy is a legal second marriage after death or divorce.

739) Before clocks, there were candle clocks that showed the passage of time by how far a candle burned. They could even be turned into an alarm clock by pushing a nail in at the desired point; the nail would fall and clank when the candle burned down to that point.

740) Yuma, Arizona, is the world's sunniest city; it averages 4,015 hours of sunshine annually, about 90% of daylight hours.

741) The Cadillac car brand was named for the founder of Detroit, Michigan. In 1701, the French explorer Antoine Laumet de la Mothe, sieur de Cadillac founded Detroit.

742) Your fingernails grow 2-3 times faster than your toenails, and the fingernails on your dominant hand tend to grow faster than on your other hand.

743) In 1917, the Seattle Metropolitans were the first U.S. hockey team to win the Stanley Cup. The Stanley Cup was first awarded in 1893.

744) Demodex mites live on your face, and you are more likely to have them the older you get. They are sausage-shaped with eight legs clustered in their front third and are up to about one-third of a millimeter long. They spend most of their time buried head down in your hair follicles; they are mostly found in our eyelids, nose, cheeks, forehead, and chin. They like areas that have a lot of oils, which is why they prefer the face. They can leave the hair follicles and slowly walk around on the skin, especially at night as they try to avoid light. The mites are transferred from person to person through contact with hair, eyebrows, and the sebaceous glands of the face. They eat, crawl, and reproduce on your face; the entire cycle from reproduction through death is about two weeks.

745) The ancient Romans called early Christians atheists because they didn't worship pagan gods.

746) Bill Clinton, George W. Bush, and Donald Trump were all born in 1946, the only year three future presidents were born.

747) Saffron is made from crocus flowers; only the stigma part of the flower is used. It takes 70,000 to 250,000 flowers to make one pound of saffron, which is why it is so expensive.

748) Only one person in modern recorded history has been struck dead by a meteorite. In 2016 in India, a 40-year-old man was relaxing outside on the grounds of a small engineering college when there was the sound of an explosion; he was found next to a two-foot crater and later succumbed to injuries sustained.

749) The Egyptian pyramids were built by paid laborers, not slaves.

750) There are multiple times more deaths caused by taking selfies each year than there are by shark attacks.

751) Each minute, an adult male human loses about 96 million cells that are replaced by cells dividing.

752) Sharks have a very well-developed sense of hearing. Their ears are small holes on the sides of their head that lead directly to the inner ear. They are particularly good at hearing low-frequency noises, such as an injured fish would make, and at finding out where a noise is coming from.

753) There are far more fake flamingos than there are real ones. There are just under 2 million flamingos in the wild; there are many millions of plastic ones.

754) The earth orbits around the sun at 66,600 mph.

755) The wheel was invented in about 3500 BC.

756) The cockroach is possibly the largest methane producer relative to its body size; they emit up to 43 times their weight in methane annually.

757) Joseph A. Walker was the first person to fly into space twice; he did it in 1963 aboard an X-15 winged aircraft. Space is defined as 62 miles above the earth.

758) Miami is the only major U.S. city founded by a woman. Julia Tuttle was a businesswoman and the original owner of the land where Miami was built.

759) According to suffragette Susan B. Anthony, the bicycle had "done more to emancipate women than anything else in the world."

760) By area, Saudi Arabia is the largest country that doesn't have any natural rivers; it is the 12th largest country.

761) Five rivers in the world are over 3,000 miles long: Nile, Amazon, Yangtze, Yellow, and Parana.

762) Ohio has the only non-rectangular state flag; it is a swallowtail shape.

763) Mapmakers have a long tradition of putting slight inaccuracies in their maps to catch people who may try to copy their work. Typically, it is something small, like a nonexistent dead-end, fake river bend, or adjusted

mountain elevation. However, in one case, a mapmaker put in the fictional town of Agloe, New York. When a store was built in the corresponding location, the owner read the map and named it Agloe General Store, assuming that was a real area name, so a fictional location became real.

764) On average, the Netherlands has the world's tallest people, with an average of 5'11 1/2" for men and 5'6 1/2" for women.

765) Most artificial banana flavoring is based on an older variety of banana that is no longer grown in bulk, so it doesn't taste very similar to the bananas you eat. The bananas you eat today are mostly the Cavendish variety, but banana flavoring is based on the Gros Michel, a sweeter variety. The Gros Michel is no longer grown in bulk because it is susceptible to a fungus.

766) The words bulb, angel, and month have no rhyming words in the English language.

767) Humans and dogs are the only two animal species known to seek visual clues from another animal's eyes, and dogs only do it with humans.

768) Forty is the only number spelled out in English that has its letters in alphabetical order.

769) About 90% of the coal we burn today came about because wood-eating bacteria didn't evolve until about 60 million years after trees existed. For tens of millions of years, all the dead tree material remained intact; trees would fall on top of each other, and the weight of the wood would compress the trees into peat and then into coal. Had wood-eating bacteria been around, they would have broken the carbon bonds and released carbon and oxygen into the air; instead, the carbon remained in the wood. Adding to the coal formation, early trees were tall, up to 160 feet, with thin trunks, fernlike leaves on top, and very shallow roots, so they fell over very easily. This era from 359 to 299 million years ago is known as the Carboniferous Period because of the large amounts of coal formed.

770) Danny Ainge is the only person named a first-team high school All-American in football, basketball, and baseball. He went to high school in Eugene, Oregon, and went on to play professional baseball for the Toronto Blue Jays and won two NBA championships with the Boston Celtics.

771) There is enough water in Lake Superior to cover all the land in North and South America in one foot of water.

772) Seven basketball players have won NCAA, Olympic, and NBA championships: Clyde Lovellette, Bill Russell, K.C. Jones, Jerry Lucas, Quinn Buckner, Michael Jordan, and Magic Johnson.

773) According to research, zebras likely evolved stripes to avoid biting flies. In an experiment, horses wearing a striped pattern coat had far fewer flies land on them than horses wearing a solid color coat. The flies spent the same amount of time circling, but far fewer landed with stripes.

774) Toilet water in the Southern Hemisphere does not rotate in the opposite direction, compared to the Northern Hemisphere, due to the Coriolis effect. The Coriolis force is a real effect and is why large systems, like hurricanes, rotate in different directions in the two hemispheres, but it is proportional to velocity, and its effect on a toilet flushing is minuscule, compared to the water jets and other irregularities.

775) According to the Bible, Goliath was six cubits tall, about nine feet.

776) The Great Barrier Reef is the world's largest living structure. Situated off the northeastern coast of Australia, it stretches for 1,429 miles and covers approximately 133,000 square miles.

777) The average major league baseball lasts for six pitches.

778) The Bluetooth wireless technology is named after King Harald "Bluetooth" Gormsson, the 10th-century ruler of Denmark.

779) McDonald's uses over 10% of the potatoes harvested in the United States annually.

780) The Jeep name comes from the army where "general purpose" was abbreviated as G.P. and phonetically translates to Jeep.

781) Camels store water in their bloodstream, not in their hump; they can drink up to 20 gallons at a time. The hump is mostly fat and serves as an alternative energy source and helps regulate body temperature. By concentrating fat in the hump, as opposed to being spread over their body, they are better able to handle hot climates.

782) Almost one-third of the world's languages are only spoken in Africa.

783) Treason, piracy, and counterfeiting are the only three crimes mentioned in the U.S. Constitution.

784) As a defense mechanism when threatened, sea cucumbers can eviscerate themselves and shoot out their internal organs. Sea cucumbers are echinoderms, which also include marine animals like starfish and sea urchins; depending on the species, they can shoot the organs out of their head or butt, but they can regrow the organs. Through a process called dedifferentiation, certain cells in their bodies lose their specialized functions and move around the sea cucumber's body and become whatever type of cell is needed to regrow the lost organs.

785) Queen Elizabeth II doesn't have a passport because passports are issued in her name and on her authority, so it would be superfluous for her to have one.

786) In 1889, Germany was the first country to introduce old-age pensions.

787) Human boogers are just dried mucus. Most mucus is swept by the nose cilia hair to the back of the throat, but near your nostrils, it can begin to dry out first and become too thick to be swept by the cilia. If it sits long enough, it dries further and becomes a booger.

788) Golf balls were originally made of wood. In the early 17th century, wood was replaced by boiled feathers compressed inside a stitched leather cover.

789) Frozen seawater contains only about one-tenth of the salt content found in liquid seawater because most of the salt separates from the water as it freezes. Due to the salt content, seawater freezes at about 28.4 degrees Fahrenheit.

790) Caterpillars essentially dissolve themselves to become butterflies. In the cocoon, the caterpillar releases enzymes that dissolve all its tissues; it then begins rapid cell division to form an adult butterfly or moth.

791) Cats are such picky eaters because they seem to be naturally driven to eat foods with about equal energy from protein and fat. They will seek out these ratios, even overriding taste preferences; science has no idea how they know what food provides the correct ratio.

792) Since she was still married to her former husband, President Andrew Jackson's wife was technically a bigamist. In 1790, his wife had separated from her first husband, but she never finalized the divorce before marrying Jackson. Once the divorce was finalized in 1794, she remarried Jackson.

793) Because the moon rotates on its axis at the same rate that it orbits the earth, only one side of the moon is visible from the earth; this is known as synchronous rotation or tidal locking.

794) Four state capitals are named after presidents: Lincoln, Jefferson City, Jackson, and Madison.

795) When Thomas Jefferson sent Lewis and Clark on their expedition, he asked them to look for wooly mammoths; Jefferson believed there might be wooly mammoths still living in the west.

796) Eighty percent of the world's population eats insects as part of their regular diet.

797) Thomas Andrews, one of the designers of the *Titanic*, was on board when it sank, and his body was never recovered. His suggestions that the ship should have 46 lifeboats instead of 20, a double hull, and a larger number of watertight bulkheads were overruled.

798) The 10,000-ton meteor that struck Russia in 2013 had an estimated impact energy of 500 kilotons and affected a 77,000 square mile area. The atomic bomb dropped on Hiroshima was about 33 times smaller.

799) It would take 1.2 million mosquitoes, each sucking once, to drain the average human of all their blood.

800) Adjusted for inflation, *Gone with the Wind* is the all-time highest-grossing movie in the United States; it is followed by *Star Wars*, *The Sound of Music*, *E.T. the Extra-Terrestrial*, and *Titanic*.

801) Graham crackers are named after 19th-century evangelical minister Sylvester Graham. He believed that food influenced libido, so he advised a bland diet to suppress lust. He espoused a coarsely ground wheat flour that became known as graham flour and later gave graham crackers their name.

802) Almost 100% of Iceland's domestic electricity production is from renewable sources, and about 85% of its overall energy consumption is from renewable sources, the highest of any country.

803) Scientists believe the world's most abundant vertebrate (animal with a backbone) species is the bristlemouth fish. They are small, deep-sea fish that are only about 3 inches long and live at depths from 3,000 feet to 3 miles. They likely number in the quadrillions.

804) The little paper tail sticking out of a Hershey's Kiss is called a niggly wiggly.

805) Eighteen countries don't have any natural rivers: Bahamas, Bahrain, Comoros, Kiribati, Kuwait, Maldives, Malta, Marshall Islands, Monaco, Nauru, Oman, Qatar, Saudi Arabia, Tonga, Tuvalu, United Arab Emirates, Vatican City, and Yemen.

806) By picking up chemical signals from human sweat, dogs can smell human fear.

807) In 1946, Nutella was invented by an Italian pastry maker looking for a cheaper alternative to chocolate that was in short supply due to WWII, so he mixed hazelnuts with some cocoa.

808) Popcorn was the first food ever microwaved on purpose. In 1945, Raytheon patented the first microwave oven; engineer Percy Spencer had first discovered the heating powers of microwaves when he accidentally melted a candy bar in his pocket. He tested it out officially on popcorn, which was a success, and on an egg, which exploded.

809) In space, the mucus that normally empties through your nose and drains down the throat backs up in the sinuses due to the lack of gravity. The only way to get rid of it is to blow your nose.

810) In 1952, Mr. Potato Head was the first toy advertised on U.S. television.

811) Pocahontas is buried along England's Thames River; she died during a visit to England.

812) Cats have more than 100 vocal sounds; dogs only have about 10.

813) The world's largest national park is in Greenland. The Northeast Greenland National Park is 375,000 square miles; it is over 100 times bigger than Yellowstone National Park and bigger than all but 29 countries. It only has about 500 visitors per year.

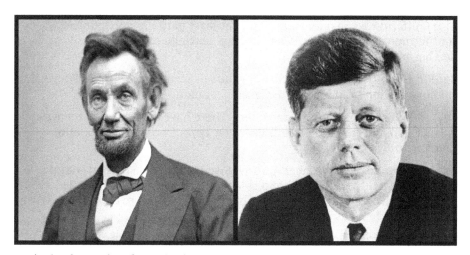

814) Abraham Lincoln and John F. Kennedy share some striking similarities, although a century apart. Lincoln was elected to Congress in 1846; Kennedy was elected to Congress in 1946. Lincoln became President in 1860; Kennedy became president in 1960. Both were assassinated on a Friday and were sitting next to their wives when it happened, and both were succeeded by a vice president named Johnson. Vice President Andrew Johnson was born in 1808; Vice President Lyndon Johnson was born in 1908.

815) Albert Einstein described it as "spooky action at a distance" and didn't believe nature would be so unreasonable, but quantum entanglement that occurs when two particles are inextricably linked together, no matter their physical separation, has been proven repeatedly. Although entangled particles are not physically connected, they are still able to share information instantaneously, breaking the rule that no information can be transmitted faster than the speed of light. In tests, entangled particles 750 miles apart have shown that any change in one is instantly reflected in the other; this would be true even if they were separated by light-years.

816) On average, Indonesia has the world's shortest people, with an average of 5'2" for men and 4'10" for women.

817) A polar bear's skin is black.

818) The first video game console was the 1972 Magnavox Odyssey. It was five years before the first Atari and 13 years before the first Nintendo; it had no sound or color and came with 28 games, including hockey, roulette, western shootout, and table tennis.

819) California is the only state that is at least partially north of the southernmost part of Canada and at least partially south of the northernmost point of Mexico.

820) In the 18th and 19th centuries, squirrels were popular pets. They were sold in pet shops and were a preferred pet among the wealthy.

821) It does snow in the Sahara Desert. There have been three recorded episodes of significant snowfall: February 1979, December 2016, and January 2018.

822) Until Sunday, September 3, 1967, Sweden drove on the left-hand side. The conversion to the right-hand side was done at 5 p.m. As people switched sides, all traffic stopped. The time and day were chosen to prevent as many accidents as possible.

823) At 1,479 miles long, Alaska is the longest state from north to south.

824) About 12% of people dream entirely in black and white. The exposure to color television seems to have had a significant impact on whether people dream in color; people who grew up with little access to color television dream in black and white about 25% of the time. In the 1940s before color television, the numbers were reversed, with about 75% of people reporting they dreamed in black and white.

825) The tallest married couple ever were Canadian Anna Haining Swan, who was 7'11", and American Martin Van Buren Bates, who was 7'9". The couple was married in 1871, and Swan later gave birth to a 22-pound baby.

826) Lake Maracaibo, Venezuela, has the most lightning strikes of any place in the world. Lightning storms occur about 10 hours a night, 140 to 160 nights a year, for a total of about 1.2 million lightning discharges per year.

827) Nepal is the only country that doesn't have either a rectangular or square flag; it has a combination of two triangular pennants.

828) Dung beetles can navigate based on the position of the moon, sun, and stars. Researchers have found that they take a mental snapshot of the night sky and use it to find their way around. The beetles can recall their exact position, and when presented with an artificial sky, they change their course accordingly.

829) Pierre, South Dakota, is the only state capital that doesn't share any letters with its state.

830) Adult domestic cats spend up to 50% of their waking time grooming.

831) Dysania is the state of finding it hard to get out of bed in the morning.

832) The Twinkie filling flavor was originally banana cream.

833) Hawaii has an average annual rainfall of 63.7 inches, the most of any state.

834) A butt is an actual volume measurement unit for wine; a buttload of wine is 126 U.S. gallons.

835) Rats don't sweat; they regulate their temperature by constricting or expanding blood vessels in their tails.

836) If you hear thunder about 15 seconds after seeing lightning, the lightning is about 3 miles away. Sound travels about one mile in five seconds.

837) The word stymie originated in golf. Until 1952 when the rules were changed, balls had to remain in place, so you could be stymied by having another player's ball between your ball and the hole; you had to loft your ball over the other ball.

838) Humans domesticated the horse around 4500 BC; the saddle was invented as early as 800 BC, but the stirrup probably wasn't created until about 300 BC.

839) The average lightning bolt is about five miles long and one inch wide.

840) Sudan has more pyramids than any other country; it has almost twice as many as Egypt.

841) One in 10,000 people has perfect pitch, the ability to identify a musical note just by hearing it with no reference note.

842) The Mississippi River flows through more states than any other river; it flows through or along 10 states: Arkansas, Illinois, Iowa, Kentucky, Louisiana, Minnesota, Mississippi, Missouri, Tennessee, and Wisconsin.

843) There are an estimated 10,000,000,000,000,000,000 (10 quintillion) insects alive at any given time.

844) In 1990, Pakistan's Benazir Bhutto was the first elected head of a nation to give birth in office.

845) A newborn Bactrian camel doesn't have any humps. Baby camels don't get their humps until they start eating solid food.

846) The creature that most people identify as a daddy longlegs spider is not a spider at all; it is a long-legged harvestman, which is an arachnid but is not a spider. Harvestmen have one body section instead of the two spiders have, two eyes instead of eight, a segmented body instead of unsegmented, no silk, no venom, and a different respiratory system than spiders, among other differences.

847) You would swim the same speed through syrup as you do through water; the additional drag is canceled out by the additional force generated from each stroke.

848) In humans, night owls tend to have higher IQs and be more creative; they are also mentally alert for a longer portion of the day than early birds.

849) The vinculum is the line between two numbers in a fraction.

850) Maryland is the only state with no natural lakes.

851) Quito, Ecuador, is closer to the equator than any other national capital city; it is 15.9 miles south of the equator.

852) The Eiffel Tower wasn't intended to be permanent. In 1909, it was scheduled for demolition, but it was saved to be used as a radio tower.

853) A group of cats is called a clowder.

854) By area, Lake Michigan is the largest lake entirely within the United States. It is 22,406 square miles.

855) Arabic numerals originated in India in the 6th or 7th century.

856) At 92 feet below sea level, Baku, Azerbaijan, is the lowest elevation national capital city.

857) Venus and Uranus are the only two planets in our solar system that rotate clockwise.

858) SOS doesn't stand for "save our ship" or anything else; it was selected as a distress signal because it is easy to transmit: three dots, three dashes, three dots.

859) Scorpions can live up to six days without air; they can also go up to a year without eating.

860) The original Peeping Tom was looking at Lady Godiva.

861) Congress allocated $2,500 for Meriwether Lewis and William Clark's expedition across America that lasted from May 1804 to September 1806.

862) When cicadas come in contact with spores of the Massospora fungus, a psychoactive plant, the fungus grows throughout the insect, consuming

its organs and converting the rear third of its body into a mass of spores. The psychoactive nature of the fungus causes the cicada to act as if nothing unusual has happened.

863) If sound waves could travel through space as they do through air, you would hear the sun burning at a volume of about 100 decibels, the same volume as a chainsaw or jackhammer. Sound intensity decreases with distance, so the 93 million miles to the sun have a large impact on the volume.

864) Mosquitoes like blood type O the most. They prefer it twice as much as type A; type B is their second choice.

865) The small bump on the inner corner of your eye is the caruncula.

866) Writer H.G. Wells coined the term "atomic bomb" over 30 years before the first atomic bomb test.

867) Grover Cleveland is the only U.S. president to serve two non-consecutive terms; he was the 22nd and 24th president.

868) After an accident during the race, Tanzanian John Akhwari ran the last 14 miles of the 1968 Olympic marathon with a dislocated knee. When asked later why he kept going, he said, "My country did not send me 9,000 miles to start the race; they sent me 9,000 miles to finish the race." He finished more than an hour behind the winner and was hailed as an Olympic hero and a symbol of the spirit of the games.

869) A rat's front teeth grow 4½ to 5½ inches each year; like other rodents, they wear them down by gnawing.

870) In an average lifetime, human skin completely replaces itself 900 times.

871) In 1999, NASA estimated that antimatter cost $28 quadrillion per pound to produce.

872) In 1841, Edgar Allan Poe created mystery fiction's first detective in *The Murders in the Rue Morgue.*

873) The tortoise is the longest living land animal of any kind; the oldest known lived to 250.

874) About 82% of the world's population has never flown on an airplane.

875) Australia has the world's highest gambling rate; over 80% of adults gamble in some form.

876) Christ's name translated directly from Hebrew to English would be Joshua; Jesus comes about by translating Hebrew to Greek to Latin to English.

877) The sooty shearwater has the world's longest distance migration. It is a common seabird and has been tracked electronically migrating 40,000 miles.

878) When the Persians were at war with the Egyptians, they rounded up and released as many cats as they could on the battlefield. Knowing the Egyptians reverence for cats, they knew they would not want to do anything to hurt the cats; the Persians won the battle.

879) In Victorian London, people were paid to collect dog poop for use in tanning leather.

880) John F. Kennedy had a lifelong struggle with back pain and was wearing a tightly laced back brace that may have kept him from recoiling to the floor of his car after he was hit with the first bullet and made him an easier target for the second shot. The brace was a firmly bound corset around his hips and lower back and higher up; he tightly laced it and put a wide Ace bandage in a figure eight around his trunk, so his movement was significantly restricted.

881) Millard Fillmore was the last U.S. president who wasn't either a Democrat or Republican; he was a member of the Whig party.

882) Scientists believe that it rains diamonds on Jupiter and Saturn. Lightning storms turn methane into soot that under pressure hardens into chunks of graphite and then diamond as it falls. The largest diamonds would likely be about a centimeter in diameter and would eventually melt in the hot planet's core.

883) The chemical thought to be responsible for old people's smell is 2-nonenal; its production increases with age, starting at about age 40.

884) Hawaii essentially has its own time zone. It is in the Hawaii-Aleutian Time Zone that includes Hawaii and Alaska's Aleutian Islands west of 169.5 degrees west longitude.

885) When it started, Starbucks only sold whole roasted coffee beans.

886) Divorce is still illegal in the Philippines and Vatican City.

887) The United States has more tornadoes than any other country.

888) Hippos sleep in the water; they surface automatically and breathe without waking up.

889) The classic film *It's a Wonderful Life* originated from a Christmas card. Philip Van Doren Stern had written a short story, *The Greatest Gift*, and had unsuccessfully tried to get it published. He sent it out as a 21-page Christmas card to his closest friends; a producer at RKO Pictures got hold of it and purchased the movie rights.

890) There is a chunk of Africa stuck under the United States. When the supercontinent Pangaea broke apart about 250 million years ago, a chunk of Africa was left behind; it is located near Alabama, just off the coast.

891) *The Simpsons* is the longest-running U.S. scripted primetime show ever; it started in 1989.

892) President Gerald Ford was once a fashion model; in the 1940s, he worked for *Cosmopolitan* and *Look* magazines.

893) In 1894, boxing was the first sport to be filmed.

894) Antarctica is the driest continent; it only gets about eight inches of precipitation annually and is considered a desert.

895) President Richard Nixon was the target of an assassination plot that involved taking over a jet and crashing it into the White House. Samuel

Byck successfully managed to take over a Delta Airlines plane, but he didn't get it off the ground. He planned to have the pilots fly it close to the White House where he would take over and crash the plane.

896) Q is the only letter that doesn't appear in any state name.

897) The ancient Romans used human urine to wash clothes.

898) Baby porcupines are called porcupettes.

899) In 1990, Nicaragua's Violeta Chamorro became the first elected female head of state in the Western Hemisphere.

900) In Germany, there is no punishment for a prisoner who tries to escape if no other laws are broken. They assume the desire for freedom is natural.

901) The Monday before and the Wednesday after the MLB All-Star game are the only two days during the year where there are no MLB, NFL, NHL or NBA games played. The MLB All-Star game is always played on a Tuesday, and there are no MLB games the day before or after, and MLB is the only professional sport played in July.

902) About 98% of all the atoms in a human body are replaced every year.

903) FDA regulations allow a certain amount of foreign animal matter to be present in food. For raisins, 10 insects and 35 fruit fly eggs per 8 ounces are acceptable; for peanut butter, 5 rodent hairs and 150 bug fragments in 1 pound is fine.

904) In 1913, Adolf Hitler, Sigmund Freud, Marshal Tito, Leon Trotsky, and Joseph Stalin all lived in Vienna within walking distance of each other.

905) Rats are not likely to blame for transmitting the Black Death bubonic plague that wiped out one-third of Europe's population in the 14th century. Experiments assessing the transmission routes prove that the parasites carrying the disease were much more likely to have come from human fleas and lice.

906) Underneath their scales, Komodo dragons have a layer of tiny bones from head to tail that protects them like chain mail or armor.

907) Captain Morgan rum is named after the 17th century Welsh privateer Sir Henry Morgan. A privateer is essentially a pirate who is sanctioned by the government; he was hired by the British to protect their interests in the Caribbean from the Spanish.

908) The Incas first domesticated guinea pigs and used them for food, sacrifices, and household pets.

909) Australia's coastline is over 16,000 miles long, and it has over 10,000 beaches, more than any other country.

116

910) The ostrich is the fastest two-legged animal; it can reach speeds over 40 mph.

911) In 1958, Mao Zedong, founding father of the People's Republic of China, initiated a campaign to eliminate sparrows that led to the deaths of 45 million people. He considered sparrows a pest, and through the Great Sparrow Campaign, he ordered all sparrows to be killed. In 1961, up to 45 million people starved to death because the elimination of sparrows led to an explosion in the insect population that ate all the crops.

912) Scientists have proven that plants can learn and remember. Mimosa pudica, an exotic herb native to South America and Central America, was trained by repeatedly dropping water on it. The Mimosa plants stopped closing their leaves when they learned that there was no damaging consequence. The plants acquired the learned behavior in seconds, and they were able to remember what had been learned for several weeks. Plants lack brains and neural tissues, but they have a sophisticated calcium-based signaling network in their cells, like an animal's memory processes.

913) Cats are crepuscular animals, which means that they are active primarily during twilight hours, just after dawn and before dusk.

914) The three-line symbol you typically find in the upper corner of a screen that you click or tap to get to a menu is called the hamburger button because it looks like a hamburger.

915) Giraffes can't cough because their lungs are too far away from their epiglottis, and coughing is a combination movement of the lungs and epiglottis.

916) More than half of the world's population lives within a 2,500-mile diameter circle in southeastern Asia. The circle incorporates 19 countries and 22 of the 37 cities in the world with a population of 10 million or more.

917) Birds are essentially immune to the heat of chili peppers; they don't have the right type or number of taste receptors to be affected.

918) Fylfot is the heraldic name for the symbol that was later known as the swastika.

919) Trees can tell if a deer is trying to eat them and defend themselves by producing astringent tannins that taste bad and put the deer off. When a bud is damaged, the tree can sense the animal's saliva in the wound, which triggers a hormone that causes it to increase the concentration of tannins in that part of the tree. It also spurs the tree to produce more growth hormones that cause the remaining buds to grow more vigorously and make up for those that have been lost to the deer.

920) Worldwide, the average human body has a volume of about 2.22 cubic feet.

921) If you define a mountain as an elevation of 2,000 feet or more, 13 states don't have any mountains: Delaware, Florida, Illinois, Indiana, Iowa, Louisiana, Michigan, Mississippi, Missouri, New Jersey, Ohio, Rhode Island, and Wisconsin.

922) Antarctica has an average elevation of 8,200 feet, the highest of any continent.

923) A cluster of 10-20 bananas is called a hand.

924) A group of bears is called a sloth.

925) California's name comes from the Spanish legend of Queen Califa, who ruled an island called California. When Cortéz landed in Baja California, he believed he had found the island of Queen Califa, which was supposed to be populated only by women who used gold to make tools and weapons.

926) It only takes 23 people in a group to have a 50% chance that two will have the same birthday. This is known as the Birthday Paradox; the probability goes up to 99.9% with just 70 people.

927) In 1884, Mount Rushmore got its name from New York attorney Charles Edward Rushmore, who visited the Black Hills area on business. He asked a guide what the name of the mountain was, and the guide said they would name it now. The name somehow stuck.

928) South Africa's Barberton Greenstone Belt is the world's oldest mountain range. The range is 3.6 billion years old, and the highest peak is 5,900 feet.

929) The expression "worth one's salt" originated in ancient Rome because soldiers were sometimes paid in salt or given an allowance to purchase it. The word salary derives from the Latin "salarium," referring to a soldier's allowance to buy salt.

930) Walking takes about 200 muscles to take a single step.

931) On average, sharks kill 12 people annually worldwide.

932) Less than 10% of legally blind Americans can read Braille.

933) London taxi drivers must pass possibly the world's hardest test. They need to know all of London's 25,000 streets, which way they run, which are one way, and everything on them down to the smallest pub, restaurant, and shop. Drivers study for years to pass.

934) The U.S. Department of Defense is the world's largest employer.

935) The first email was sent in 1971.

936) Cerebral hypoxia is the end cause of every human death. Lack of oxygen to the brain is the final cause of death, regardless of what initiates it.

937) Czech Republic's Ester Ledecka is the first woman to win gold medals in two different sports at the same Winter Olympics. At the 2018 PyeongChang Olympics, she won in skiing and snowboarding.

938) Of all the senses, smell is most closely linked to memory.

939) In Michigan, you are never more than six miles from a body of water. Michigan has over 11,000 inland lakes plus 4 of the 5 Great Lakes.

940) Sometime between 1268 and 1300, the first pair of corrective eyeglasses were invented in Italy; they were two reading stones (magnifying glasses) connected with a hinge. They were balanced on the bridge of the nose.

941) The term "slush fund" was originally used by sailors to refer to the side money they made selling animal fat; sailors sold the fat from the meat cooked on board to tallow makers.

942) Despite being a ruthless warlord, Genghis Khan was a very enlightened ruler. He established freedom of religion, banned torture of prisoners, outlawed slavery, promoted people based on individual merit rather than birth, established universal law, created a writing system, instituted an international postal system, and redistributed the wealth he gained.

943) You can always see your nose, but you don't see it unless you think about it. The process is called unconscious selective attention and allows the brain to block out distractions.

944) In 1964, the world record for a human going without sleep was set by 17-year-old Randy Gardner; he was intentionally awake for 11 days and 25 minutes without any stimulants.

945) In case their pants split, Major League Baseball umpires are required to wear black underwear.

946) The word "robot" was first used in a 1920 play called *Rossum's Universal Robots*. It comes from the Slavic word "rabota," meaning slave labor.

947) If you've ever yawned and had saliva shoot out your mouth, it is called glecking. The salivary glands underneath your tongue become stimulated and shoot a concentrated jet of pure saliva; it typically happens when yawning.

948) Originally, the term third world country did not mean a developing country. A French demographer coined the term in 1952, during the Cold War, and it referred to countries that weren't aligned with either the United States or the Soviet Union.

949) A priest was the first person to propose the big bang origin of the universe; Georges Lemaitre's work preceded Edwin Hubble.

950) In 1968, the United States adopted the 911 emergency phone number; the first call was made in Haleyville, Alabama.

951) Human babies have 300 bones; some fuse together to form the 206 bones in adults.

952) France and its territories cover more time zones than any other country. France covers 12 time zones; the United States and Russia and their territories each cover 11 time zones.

953) In 1983, Guion Bluford was the first African American in space.

954) Founded about 2000 BC, Cholula, Mexico, is believed to be the oldest continuously inhabited North American city.

955) As is often the case, the Disney film *Pinocchio* was a much lighter take on the original story. The original does feature a talking cricket, but he isn't named Jiminy Cricket. After receiving advice he doesn't like, Pinocchio gets mad and kills the cricket. The talking cricket returns later as a ghost to give Pinocchio additional advice.

956) Venus is often called the Earth's twin because it is nearly the same size and mass and has a similar composition.

957) In 1888, the first vending machine in the United States dispensed Tutti-Frutti gum.

958) *Toy Story* (1995) was the world's first computer-animated feature film.

959) Whispering is harder on your vocal cords than normal speech.

960) The average American professional football game lasts 3 hours and 12 minutes but only has about 11 minutes when the ball is in play.

961) A combination of two words to make a new word, such as breakfast and lunch into brunch, is called a portmanteau.

962) In ancient Rome, gladiators were huge celebrities; wealthy women would buy vials of their sweat and use it as face cream.

963) Female ferrets can die if they don't mate. The female stays in heat until she mates; if she doesn't, very high levels of estrogen remain in her blood for a long time and can cause aplastic anemia and death. She doesn't have to get pregnant, but she must mate.

964) The first cell phone call was made in 1973.

965) The ostrich is the only bird with two toes on each foot.

966) You can't hum while holding your nose; to create the humming sound, air must escape through your nose.

967) Litmus paper can change color when exposed to an acid or base because it is infused with lichens.

968) Worldwide, about 24,000 people are killed by lightning annually.

969) The earth's surface curves out of sight at about 3.1 miles.

970) The earth's continental plates drift about as fast as human fingernails grow.

971) On average, the Antarctic ice sheet is one mile thick.

972) The Eiffel Tower was originally intended for Barcelona; Spain rejected the project.

973) Twelve languages are written right to left: Arabic, Aramaic, Azeri, Divehi, Fula, Hebrew, Kurdish, N'ko, Persian, Rohingya, Syriac, and Urdu.

974) Balloons were originally made from animal bladders.

975) When a woodpecker's beak hits a tree, it experiences 1,000 times the force of gravity.

976) Researchers locate penguin colonies by looking for the stain trail from their droppings via satellite. It is easier to see than looking for the penguins themselves.

977) *It Happened One Night* (1934), *One Flew Over the Cuckoo's Nest* (1975), and *The Silence of the Lambs* (1991) are the only three films to win all five major Academy Awards (best picture, director, actor, actress, and screenplay).

978) Alaska is the only state name that can be typed on one row of a standard keyboard.

979) Adjusted for inflation, *The Exorcist* is the only horror film to gross $1 billion in the United States.

980) Thomas Jefferson had the largest personal book collection in the United States and sold it to become part of the Library of Congress after the library was destroyed in the War of 1812.

981) Forks were first introduced in Italy in the 11th century; however, they were originally seen as an offense to God since they were considered artificial hands and therefore sacrilegious.

982) Until 1934, sheep grazed in New York's Central Park. For fear they would be eaten, they were moved during the Great Depression.

983) To make customers drink more, caviar was served free in old west saloons.

984) Five European countries have the same name as their capital city: Vatican City, Monaco, Luxembourg, Andorra, and San Marino.

985) When threatened, ladybugs release a foul-smelling chemical from their knees that can repulse predators. The substance is a mix of alkaloids and can also ooze from their abdomens.

986) The world's most popular first name is Mohammed and its variations.

987) Joseph Stalin plotted to kill John Wayne and sent two men to pose as FBI agents to assassinate him. Stalin was a big film fan and considered Wayne a threat to the Soviet Union because of his strong anti-communist beliefs.

988) Ancient Roman public toilets had a long marble bench with holes on top, where you sat, and holes in the front, for the sponge on a stick used to clean yourself after. There were no doors or dividing walls; you sat right next to someone else. Once you had done your business, you would rinse the sponge in the channel of running water at your feet, push the sponge on a stick through the hole in the front and wipe yourself, and then rinse off the sponge and leave it in a basin for the next person.

989) The shape of a Pringles chip is called a hyperbolic paraboloid; it allows easier stacking and reduces broken chips.

990) Queen is the only music group where every member has written more than one number-one single; all four members have been inducted into the Songwriters Hall of Fame.

991) The Chinese giant salamander is the world's largest amphibian and can be almost six feet long.

992) The short, erect tail of a hare, rabbit, or deer is called a scut.

993) The Arctic Desert is the largest desert at least partially in North America. It covers 5.4 million square miles in Canada, Greenland, Norway, Russia, Sweden, and the United States.

994) A spider's muscles pull its legs inward, but they can't push them out again. To push them out, it must pump a watery liquid into its legs.

995) Dogs tend to wag their tails more towards their right when they are relaxed and more to their left when they are afraid or insecure.

996) To produce one pound of honey, a hive of bees must visit 2 million flowers and fly about 55,000 miles. One bee colony can produce 60 to 100 pounds of honey annually. An average worker bee makes only about 1/12 of a teaspoon of honey in its lifetime and has a lifespan of about 2 months; queen bees typically live for 3 to 5 years.

997) Today's average American woman weighs as much as the average American man from the 1960s.

998) In his writings, William Shakespeare created over 1,700 of our common words and phrases, more than anyone else by far. He did it by changing nouns into verbs, changing verbs into adjectives, connecting words never used together, adding prefixes and suffixes, and creating original words. Some examples of his creations include: fancy-free, lie low, foregone conclusion, a sorry sight, for goodness sake, good riddance, mum's the word, what's done is done, scuffle, uncomfortable, manager, dishearten, eventful, new-fangled, hot-blooded, rant, with bated breath, laughable, negotiate, jaded, a wild goose chase, a heart of gold, fashionable, puking, dead as a doornail, obscene, bedazzled, addiction, faint-hearted, one fell swoop, vanish into thin air, swagger, zany, grovel, unreal, spotless reputation, full circle, arch-villain, bloodstained, and all of a sudden.

999) The Catholic church made Galileo recant his theory that the earth revolves around the sun; it took them 359 years to declare Galileo was right in 1992.

1000) At up to 150 pounds, the South American capybara is the world's largest rodent.

If you enjoyed this book and learned a little and would like others to enjoy it also, please put out a review or rating. If you scan the QR code below, it will take you directly to the Amazon review and rating page.

Made in the USA
Las Vegas, NV
10 December 2024